My ankle gave in. I stumbled forward, fighting to regain some balance. Then I crashed. The rough ground tore my skin.

Even in fourth grade I already knew the only thing worse than falling in front of my classmates was letting them see me cry, so I swallowed hard against the sobs rising in my throat.

A boy yelled, "Why do we got to have a hop-along on our team? She's nothing but a *cripple.*" Such taunts echoed through my childhood.

Today, the sneers were silenced.

When Slugger and I made our way down the hall to where Vickie, his trainer, waited, we moved slowly, awkwardly; but we moved *together.* After a lifetime of struggling to keep up with others, I found myself accompanied by an incredible dog, one willing to walk beside me at my pace.

I grinned at Vickie.

She didn't return my smile. Tears made wet, serpentine tracks down her face. Suddenly I felt as if my heart had plunged into my stomach. "What's wrong?"

"Nothing's wrong," Vickie answered. "That's just it; it's *right.*" She brushed a tear from her cheek and continued, "I know this dog, and when I see how he responds to you, there's no doubt in my mind. You two are destined to be a team. That's more than my hunch. It's something Slugger knows."

a dog named Slugger

The true story of the friend who changed my world.

Leigh Brill

Bell Bridge Books

Bell Bridge Books
PO BOX 30921
Memphis, TN 38130
ISBN: 978-0-9843256-5-8

Bell Bridge Books is an Imprint of BelleBooks, Inc.

While Slugger's story is true, some places, events, and names have been changed or combined in an effort to safeguard the privacy of the individuals involved.

We at BelleBooks enjoy hearing from readers. You can contact us at the address above or at BelleBooks@BelleBooks.com
Visit our websites – www.BelleBooks.com and www.BellBridgeBooks.com.

10 9 8 7 6 5 4 3 2

Cover design: Debra Dixon
Interior design: Hank Smith
Photo Credits: Pranav Singh

Dedication

For Slugger, and for all working dogs and their human families, who prove that service changes lives.

Acknowledgments

Years ago I promised Slugger I would share his story; the fulfillment of that promise would not have been possible without the support of many people.

My agent, Robert Astle of Robert Astle and Associates Literary Management, Inc., recognized something special in Slugger's story from the start. Thanks, Robert, for your tireless enthusiasm through all the ups and downs. I'm honored by your hard work and dedication.

I'd also like to express my deep appreciation to my editor, Deb Smith. Thank you, Deb, for your keen and sensitive insights, your sense of humor, and most of all your commitment to this book. You've helped make Slugger's story shine. Thanks also to Debra Dixon for believing in this project, and for helping make it even more beautiful than I could have imagined. Pam Ireland, Hank Smith, and the entire team at BelleBooks, you've truly given Slugger's story a home.

A special thank you to Hillel Black. Working with you was a great experience, and Slugger's story is stronger because you helped shape it. Thanks as well to David Ratner and the team at Newman Communications. You've offered the perfect mix of professionalism and enthusiasm while helping me share Slugger's story. I'm also grateful to a wonderful life coach for writers, Katey Coffing, PhD of Women-Ink.com. for her unfailing support. Thank you, Katey, for being a wise "vice gut," and remarkable friend.

I've been fortunate to be surrounded by people who inspire my words and my heart. To my family, thank you for sharing and brightening my journey. Pranav, thank you for hanging in there, for giving so much. This journey would not have been possible without you. To my dear friends Carol and Doug (and Griffin, of course), your love and laughter have helped me more than words can express. Heartfelt thanks to my friend, Laurie, too, for helping and encouraging me. I'm also grateful to the Squaw Valley Community of Writers, and especially my mentor, Joy. Thank you all for believing in my ability to tell this story even before I did.

Finally, I offer my sincere admiration and gratitude to the members of my "dog family". I'm grateful for the help and support offered by so many incredible dog trainers, veterinarians, other professionals, and volunteers over the years. Any errors in describing training methods or veterinary issues are strictly attributable to the author. Thank you to everyone who worked with Caring Canine Companions of Virginia, especially Stuart and Terry Porter, Sylvia Fisher, Vickie Polk, and Amy Skelton. Today I can't imagine a sweeter embodiment of joyfulness than I find in my beloved dog, Kenda. I'm blessed by our partnership. To those who made that partnership possible—everyone at Saint Francis Service Dogs, especially Carol and Doug Willoughby and Booker (their inspiration), to Mark, Beth, David, Catherine, and Emma Finkler, Mitzi and Jeff Tinaglia, Matt Davis, and Karen Hough—thank you all for changing my life. And thank you for proving that a gift is most beautiful when it is shared.

—Leigh

Contents

a dog
named
Slugger

Prologue

My hands were trembling again. I needed to get a quarter out of my purse, but my quivering fingers made the task feel as intricate as neurosurgery. It's always been that way with cerebral palsy—sometimes I just shake. I can't help it. Still, the tired store clerk waiting at the counter in front of me didn't understand this. She sighed, clearly wishing I would hurry up and pay for my purchase. I would have liked to be able to do that.

At last I grasped the quarter. I started to hand it to the clerk, and my fingers slipped. With a familiar flat plink, the coin hit the floor and rolled past the purple metal legs of my wheelchair. It was far beyond my reach now, but I knew what to do. I spoke softly to the companion who was standing attentively at my side, and he did what I could not. He retrieved the wayward quarter and put it carefully on the counter before taking his place beside me once more. I smiled when he did this. Now the tired clerk was smiling too. "How amazing!" she exclaimed. "I never knew a dog could do that!"

My Labrador, Slugger, flicked his tongue across his jowls as if to remove the taste of the quarter. He was a highly trained service dog; for him, scooping a fallen coin into his mouth—and then spitting it out on command—was routine. Slugger was accustomed to retrieving anything that slipped from my grasp. My canine partner also carried my belongings, fetched my telephone, and opened heavy doors for me. His unwavering devotion brought me confidence and joy. With Slugger by my side, I discovered the life-changing power of unconditional love. And I learned that even the most formidable challenges can offer something good.

Chapter 1

Six Years Earlier

I Need Help

The scarlet oak and white ash groaned on that October afternoon in 1992. Lashed by a bitter wind, even the stateliest trees on the campus of James Madison University creaked as if lamenting the frigid gusts in their boughs. *I'll bet that's how my bones sound,* I thought as I walked to my graduate class. At twenty-two, I knew Virginia's cold autumn weather would make the symptoms of my congenital cerebral palsy much worse—it always had. But I wasn't going to dwell on it. I had just begun working toward my masters in community agency counseling, and I wanted to focus on my coursework. Obsessing over my studies made it easier to ignore the pain of my condition and the newest stress fractures in my feet. I hunched beneath my overstuffed backpack and willed myself to keep going.

The sidewalks were full of pushy bodies on

strong, hurrying legs; and I avoided them whenever possible. The lawn seemed a safer route. It was less crowded. Trekking across the grass, I headed to my Abnormal Psychology class. I'd had trouble cramming two notebooks, my textbook, and the fourth edition of the *Diagnostic and Statistical Manual of Mental Disorders (DSM)* into my purple backpack. Now the load banged against me as I walked. Even with the top unzipped so that the flaps parted in a black-toothed grin, my pack was straining at the seams. My body was straining too, though I refused to acknowledge this.

Beneath my feet, the earth was furrowed. This was dangerous terrain for legs like mine. I should have been paying close attention to where I put my feet, but the icy wind stole my attention. It stung my face and turned my fingers numb 'round the edges.

I shoved my left hand deep into the pocket of my winter coat and felt my fuzzy yellow mittens there. But I couldn't make my half-frozen fingers grasp them. The mittens popped from my pocket and fell to the ground. "Great," I mumbled, bending to retrieve them. I should have squatted down carefully. I should have moved slowly to keep my balance on the uneven ground. Instead, I dove forward, mimicking the start of an impromptu somersault.

Suddenly my body was out of control. I slammed against the earth so hard that my breath deserted me. I tried to inhale. It was like sucking a thick milkshake through a cracked straw. The effort made me dizzy, and each attempt brought more pain than air. I smelled dirt, tasted its grittiness on my lips.

With my face turned sideways and my head flat to

the ground, I resembled a kid pressing an ear against the metal snake of a railroad track in hopes of hearing an oncoming train. But I was too shaken to hear anything. The steady whir and click of an approaching mountain bike went unnoticed until its rider's words exploded behind me. "Whoa, perfect ten! Way to go, grace!" The voice was taunting, sarcastic. I looked up in time to see a flash of spandex, bright blue leggings over sculpted calf muscles. Those muscles flexed and pumped. They did not slow as the rider pedaled past me.

"Shut up!" I wheezed. Without air, my response collapsed, as empty as a deflated balloon. But the voice inside my mind was clear now; it took up a familiar mantra, *Just try to relax. The sooner you do, the sooner the pain will leave.*

I'd first heard this when I was just eight years old. I was in the hospital then, facing one of the many surgeries that marked my childhood. An orderly had helped me onto a stretcher. It was cozy and the blankets were warm, so I didn't protest when my arms and legs were strapped down. I was wheeled into a large waiting room where other boys and girls lay on their own cots. A nurse moved, catlike, among them. Suddenly she was poised over me. She looked as if she might pounce, but instead she rolled me onto my side. My hospital gown—a parade of cheerful teddy bears marching across yellow fabric—fell away and I blushed. A sharp sting on my bottom made me cry. The nurse patted my shoulder reassuringly. "Try to relax, honey. The sooner you do, the sooner the pain will go away."

The familiar edges of my reality slowly melted like butter in the sun. My father's face, my mother's voice, the sheets pressed against my body, everything began to quiver as I was wheeled into the operating room. This was a vast place of shining metal and blue-green tiles. The inhabitants were blue-green too. In their caps and masks and suits, they looked like grotesque turtles. Later I would have nightmares about those turtles. *Who were they? What did they want? What were they going to do to me?*

Unknown hands loosened the straps around my arms and legs. *Were they going to let me go? Oh God, please make them let me go. Please!* I was lifted onto a metal table. The biggest light I'd ever seen was suspended just above me. It was so bright I couldn't look at it, but I felt its heat against my skin. Gloved fingers spread cold gel on my chest and placed two small white discs there. *Why?*

Suddenly a figure leaned close to me, and I heard the familiar voice of my doctor. "Hi there, Leigh. Just relax now. We put those patches on so we can listen to your heart. Hear that noise that sounds like a train? That's your heart doing its job." I tried to tell my doctor that I didn't care about the train in my chest, that I only wanted to get out of there, but I couldn't make my lips work.

A black rubber mask hovered above my face like a predatory insect. As it moved closer and closer, I smelled a horrible odor. My stomach lurched. I tried to turn away, to swallow a gulp of clean air, but a gloved hand held my head still. "It's time for you to go to sleep," a nurse said. She caressed my cheek then. "Breathe easy, Leigh. Just try to relax."

Now, crumpled against the ground years later, I tried to heed those words, to stay calm. Slowly I sat up. I used my mittens to dust off my face and hair. The force of my fall had sent everything sailing from my backpack. I gathered my belongings carefully, plucking pens from the grass, shaking dirt from the pages of my notebooks. The maroon cover of my *DSM* was torn—a white line zigzagged its way down the middle. With trembling hands I slid the damaged book gingerly into my backpack. I vowed to fix it as soon as possible. My chest ached fiercely, my left wrist throbbed, my hands were scraped and bleeding. And I was wondering where I could find some tape to mend the cover of my book.

Swallowing hard, I picked myself up and limped to my class. The professor, a red-faced man with close-set eyes, stood at the chalkboard drawing a diagram of psychiatric disorders. When I entered, he paused. He turned to scowl at me. "This class begins at 4:00, not 4:15."

"Sorry I'm late." I apologized without meaning it and slid into the first empty desk I saw.

Frantically copying the diagram into my notebook, I pushed my emotions—the pain, the anger, the sense of powerlessness—to the back of my mind. I didn't want to feel them. But later that night I had no choice. The long hours of darkness brought agonizing pain. With clusters of aspirin on my tongue and heating pads wrapped 'round my feet, I realized I couldn't deny it anymore. The truth slipped past the fear in my throat. It came out, a choked whisper in the dark: *I need help.*

The next morning I scheduled an appointment with a new doctor. When I arrived at his office several days later, the silver-haired specialist told me not to worry. He said I was so beautiful that I wouldn't have any trouble finding a nice man to take care of me. I bristled. *What does a nice man have to do with the pain in my feet?* I thought. *And who says I can't take care of myself?* But the doctor grasped my hand suddenly and my questions remained unspoken. His tone was soft, as if he were cooing to an infant. "Your body can no longer do what you're asking it to do. You need to get a wheelchair."

I yanked my hand back. *No!* the voice inside me declared. *I won't!*

I'd struggled to be just like everyone else for as long as I could remember, even as a little girl growing up on my grandfather's farm in Virginia's Shenandoah Valley. Pop Pop's barn was the sanctuary of my childhood. I loved to wander through the cattle stalls and explore every dark and musty corner. Sometimes I discovered other refugees in the barn; feral mama cats often birthed and raised their young amid the stored hay. I'd follow the faint mews that rose from their hidden nurseries and crawl over prickly hay bales until I found them. Then, in the moment of discovery, my mind would fill with such awe that I'd forget even to breathe. The tiny creatures I'd found seemed to stop breathing, too. They simply stared up at me, fragile and exposed; their eyes, like newly lit beacons, gleamed with alarm.

When I was little, I often felt like those barn

kittens. Terrified of being discovered, I worried that other people would see just how messed up I was. I didn't know how to face my fear then. I couldn't even name it. So I did the only thing I knew how to do. I devoted myself to the appearance and pursuit of normalcy.

By my early twenties, I'd perfected that pursuit. Now I wondered. How can I look like everyone else if I surrender to a wheelchair? How can I be normal? Still, these questions were too big, too frightening, to utter. I simply nodded politely to the doctor and thanked him for his time.

Not until I'd paid the sunny receptionist and scrambled out of the office did I acknowledge my true feelings. Outside, I slumped against the building's brick wall, pressing my palms against its roughness to stop them from shaking. I bowed my head then and squeezed my eyes shut as if a moment's blindness might hold back a reality I was too terrified to see. "Please God," I whispered. "Help me find another answer, one that's right for me."

Chapter 2

An Unexpected Answer

Weeks later—still waiting for that answer—I was trudging from the campus library to my dorm when a familiar voice called, "Hiya, Leigh!" My friend and classmate, Steve, was sitting on a nearby bench with a woman I didn't recognize. He waved and motioned for me to come over.

"Hey! How's it going?" I said, puffing slightly as I joined them.

"Not bad," Steve nodded, then continued, "Leigh, I don't think you've met Anne Cooper, have you?" He gestured to the woman beside him. "She's just joined our program and is signed up for lots of the same classes."

"It's nice to meet you, Anne!" I said. "Welcome to the wonderful world of community agency counseling."

"Yeah, thanks," Anne answered with a laugh. I grinned back at her. That's when I noticed my new classmate sparkled; even her metal crutches gleamed.

Her long hair was pulled back on each side, held in place by pretty, painted barrettes. Her burgundy blouse complemented the autumn hues of her corduroy skirt; and over every inch of her perfectly coordinated ensemble was a fine layer of auburn fur. It stuck like pixie dust.

The tiny hairs apparently came from a big dog lying beneath the bench. The animal had been so still when I'd approached, I hadn't even spotted it at first. Now I stared outright.

Noting my gaze, Anne explained, "That's my service dog, Caesar! He's specially trained to provide mobility assistance." At the sound of his name, the dog, who resembled a lean boxer with a long snout, looked up and wagged his tail. He wore a bright green backpack and a regal expression befitting his name.

Though I'd heard of dogs guiding blind people, I didn't realize they could also be trained to assist those with other disabilities. "Wow, how neat!" I exclaimed. As a child I'd spent countless hours on my grandparents' farm. I fell in love with all the animals there. Still, I'd been closest to our family's cocker spaniel, Josie; she had always listened to me. Now I couldn't help gushing about Josie, to Anne. "I tell you that little dog came when I called, sat when I asked, and resisted the urge to jump up on me. She was brilliant!"

But not long after that first meeting, Anne's service dog redefined my concept of canine brilliance. I was sitting in my Human Memory class, scribbling notes, when it happened. My gaze kept wandering across the room. Anne was seated there with Caesar lying at her feet. Peering around sneakers and high heels, business flats, and Birkenstocks, I stared at the dog, mesmerized by the way his eyebrows twitched as he surveyed the world around him.

Suddenly Caesar jumped to his feet. I was so surprised that I nearly popped out of my chair. *What the heck is he doing?* I wondered. Now the dog's head was down. He seemed to be nudging something with his nose. I shifted in my seat to get a better view. It was a pen he was after, a fallen ballpoint with a blue lid. But the big dog wasn't simply bumping it with his nose. He was actually scooping it into his mouth. He cradled the pen carefully, without biting down. The plastic cap peeked from beneath the russet suede of his jowls. Then Caesar nuzzled Anne's hand. His tail waved as he deposited the pen into her waiting fingers.

I wanted to shout, "Holy moly, will you look at that!" Still, I knew better than to disrupt the studious decorum of the lecture hall, so I squelched my instincts and gawked in silence.

When class let out, I rushed up to Anne and her dog with the zeal of a rock-star groupie. "Caesar sure is incredible! One minute he's all chilled out and the next he's getting your pen off the floor and putting it right in your hand. And he didn't even break it, the pen I mean. Talk about smart!" I stopped babbling just long enough to take a breath.

My classmate smiled. "Yes, he is wonderful, all right. And he loves to work. This dog makes things so much easier for me." Anne spoke softly, with unhurried precision. The fingers of her left hand massaged Caesar's ear, and he tilted his head toward the pleasure.

I grinned. "That is one cool dog! You two are quite a team."

"Yes." Anne winked. "The folks at Caring Canine Companions trained him for me free of charge; and now I can't imagine life without him." She paused, looked me in the eye. "You know, if you ever want to find out about getting a service dog to help you, I could give you some information."

Me? "Oh, I'm not, I mean, I don't . . . " Denial, slick and familiar, filled my mouth. I'd always been good at pretending I was fine on my own.

Perhaps it was my left wrist, still aching from my latest fall, that stopped my lies then. Or maybe I sensed that Anne's experience with her own disability helped her see through my charade. I swallowed the words I knew so well and took a deep breath. "I'd like that." Anne handed me a tan brochure. I thanked her and tucked it into my backpack.

Hours later, sprawled across my bed, I stared at the words printed on the cover of the brochure Anne had given me: *Caring Canine Companions: specially-trained dogs to assist elderly people and those with disabilities.* "Well, I don't reckon I need help because of my age yet," I said aloud, "but maybe I could get a dog to help with the craziness."

'Craziness' wasn't a big enough name for my pain, frustration, and shame; still, it felt safer than saying 'cerebral palsy.' I flipped the brochure open. For the second time that day the words *holy moly* waited at my lips. This time I let them out.

The pamphlet held a collage of dog photographs. These weren't ordinary images with posed pooches staring in the general direction of a camera; the dogs in these pictures were doing incredible things.

In one image, a boxer held a business envelope in its mouth. A smiling woman was seated on a nearby couch, and the dog was stretching toward her extended hand as if to offer her the letter.

In another picture, a golden retriever stood a few feet from an open storefront door. There was a nylon strap attached to the dog's working harness and the opposite end was looped 'round the door handle. The dog braced its body, holding the door open, so that a man in a wheelchair could pass through.

A black dog peered out from a third image. This dog was tall and dressed in a leather harness. A rigid handle rose above the dog's haunches, and a girl's hand rested against it. Her hand was bent; her knotted fingers reached in unusual directions. But she stood beside her dog, grinning. There was an unopened bag of potato chips in her canine companion's mouth. The dog's jaws fit just over the top left corner of the package without touching the swirly *S* of the sour cream and onion label.

The final picture showed a diverse group. Some people were standing, others were seated in wheelchairs. There were bespectacled eyes, calloused hands, porcelain complexions, and shiny scalps with tufts of hair as fine as the down of an old feather pillow. Yet every person had a dog, and everyone was smiling. The caption beneath this photograph read, "Our CCC Teams."

The remaining text in the brochure was full of empowering words: *independence, companionship, improved quality of life.* On the back flap I read a single intriguing sentence: "Want to know more?" I'd been holding my breath without realizing it, and now my answer slid out on a swoosh of warm air. "Yeah!"

I picked up the telephone the next day, and though I told myself not to be nervous, my fingers shook worse than usual as I dialed the number for Caring Canine Companions. I hoped my voice wouldn't follow suit. Taking a deep breath, I counted the rings on the line, One. *Please pick up.* Two. *Please pick up.* Three. *Come on, pick . . .*

"Caring Canine Companions. This is Sylvia."

I gulped. "I have cerebral palsy, and I'd like to find out if a service dog could help me." As a child I'd been taught to keep my CP a secret. I didn't talk about it or even say its name. But now the words rushed from my mouth like a slapdash confession. Having uttered them, I felt giddy. In the seconds that followed I heard nothing but the sound of my own breathing. Then, a chuckle.

"I'm glad you're interested in getting a dog," Sylvia said, "but hang on a minute; we've got lots to talk about. Let's start with your name."

It was my turn to laugh. "Oops. My name is Leigh Brill."

"Okay, Leigh. I'm going to take some notes while we talk to help me keep track of things. First, why don't you tell me a little about yourself?"

My excitement, coupled with the release of acknowledging my disability, made me deaf to the word *little*. I launched into so detailed an account of my life that Sylvia would later tell me her hand ached for hours from taking notes on our conversation. I hardly paused long enough to breathe until one question rendered me speechless. "Leigh, what do you have trouble doing?"

I wanted to shout, "Everything!" But the voice in my head hissed, *you can't say that!* It urged my usual lie: *nothing's hard for me.* Caught between the two extremes, I blurted, "What do you mean?"

"I have to know what is hard for you to do, so I can figure out how a service dog might help," Sylvia answered.

Suddenly I understood. For the first time in my life, I didn't need to pretend, I didn't need to be just like everyone else; I only needed to be honest. I paused for a moment, considering my answer. I felt the weight and shape of it; turned it over and over like a child flipping a bit of quartz in her hand to examine every side and angle. "Well, I walk funny and my balance is bad," I said at last. "I fall a lot. My hands shake too. That means I'm not so good at carrying things. And if I drop stuff, sometimes it's hard to just bend down and get it."

It was freeing to say these things, and Sylvia's response rewarded my honesty. "It sounds like a service dog could be great for you," she said. "Why don't I send you an application? Look it over, give it some thought. If you decide this is the right thing for you, go ahead and fill out the forms and return them to me. In the meantime you can call me when you think of questions."

My application arrived the next week. I completed it the very day it showed up in my mailbox, and by the end of that week, I'd memorized the CCC phone number. Though I tried not to pester Sylvia, I often called her just to "talk dog." I pelted her with questions: What would I need to learn in order to work with a service dog? Where could the two of us go together? Would my canine assistant be male or female? What breed could I expect? And how long, oh *how* long, before I'd get a dog of my own?

Sylvia, bless her, was patient and helpful. She assured me that I'd be able to go almost anywhere with my service dog, but that would only happen after extensive instruction with my canine companion and a trainer/handler. Both male and female dogs were in the CCC program, and they included a variety of pure and mixed breeds.

Still, Sylvia couldn't tell me the specifics about my future partner yet. She said she'd have to find an animal whose personality, strengths, and energy level would be a good fit for me. My heart sank when she added, "Don't hold your breath, Leigh. Finding your perfect dog could take a year or longer."

Though disheartened by the prospect of a long wait, I began researching and talking about service dogs constantly. For months I shared the fascinating facts I discovered with family, friends, and anyone who'd listen. "Service dogs can come in all shapes and sizes, you know. And they're very smart; a good working dog can learn as many as fifty different words!"

I became so obsessed with my imminent

partnership that I did more than just talk about it. I daydreamed about it too. One afternoon during summer break, I was in the shower, washing my hair. As I watched the shampoo bubbles scuttle across the tub floor, I was thinking about how Sylvia told me that during the bonding phase of a new partnership, dog and human must be inseparable.

She'd stressed that during this part of training, my dog would need to accompany me everywhere and be with me at all times. Now I imagined that loyal canine, keeping vigil on my green bath mat, occasionally licking the water droplets that strayed down the side of the tub.

Abruptly my daydream ended, dissolved by the ringing of the telephone. With sweet-smelling froth slipping from my scalp, I splashed out of the shower and grabbed a towel. "If this is a telemarketer, I'm going to be really pissed," I growled as I performed a frantic wet-footed dance toward the phone.

"Hello, Leigh?" The greeting was Sylvia's.

Words began to push and shove in my mind the instant I recognized her voice. I wanted to ask, "Are you calling with good news?" but suddenly I was too nervous to string the words together. I stammered idiotically, "Uh, yeah, it's me."

My ear was full of shampoo, yet I could still hear the smile in Sylvia's voice when she announced, "Guess what? I think we may have found the dog for you; Slugger is a wonderful yellow Labrador!"

Sylvia continued, but I didn't catch anything else she said. All I heard was that there might be a dog for me, a dog named Slugger.

Chapter 3

Dog Day

It was four in the morning and I was too excited to sleep. Two weeks had passed since Sylvia's wonderful news; and now it was here—dog day! In a few hours I'd be meeting Slugger for the very first time.

My thoughts drifted back to one of my earliest conversations with Sylvia. She'd explained that the process of matching a service dog and human partner is like an adoption, and even with careful screening and hard work, there's no guarantee that every partnership will succeed.

In fact Sylvia told me that Slugger had progressed part way into the matching process with a woman named Diane when that potential partnership fell through. Diane used a wheelchair and had relished the idea of a canine assistant, but the busy mother of four eventually decided not to bring an 85-pound dog—even a well-trained one—into her lively household. She was, according to Sylvia, bothered by the big Lab's wagging tail.

"You're kidding! Heck, I'd *want* the dog's tail to

wag." I'd responded incredulously. Secretly I was grateful for Diane's change of heart.

In the dark and early morning—waiting to meet Slugger—that gratitude came back to me. It expanded then flowed out in a sudden fusion of laughter and tears. Many people wait years to get a service dog. Though my natural impatience made it feel as if I'd been waiting for decades, in truth only nine months had passed.

If you could hang on all those months, surely you can make it a few more hours, the voice inside me said. *Best try and get some rest now.* Yes, rest would be reasonable, wise. Still, I couldn't stop wondering about Slugger. Would he be as beautiful as I'd imagined? Would he like me? Would he listen? Would the two of us be a match?

Hours later, those same questions circled 'round inside my mind as I drove over the winding road that connected my family's mountain home to the town of Woodstock, Virginia. I would soon meet Slugger and his trainer at the public library there. Beams of sunlight reached like long and sparkling fingers, touching asphalt, clustered buildings, and verdant lawns. The brightness matched my disposition. This day was perfect!

Though I didn't realize it, my perfect day marked an end as well as a beginning. Two years before I'd heard of CCC, Sylvia had visited her friends Stuart and Terry Porter. Terry was instrumental in helping run the organization, and she and her husband also bred Labrador retrievers. Sylvia had been in search of a star puppy; when she spotted a yellow male with a gleam in his eye and enough pizzazz to merit a name like *Slugger*, she knew she'd found what she was after.

Though only a few weeks old when Sylvia met him, Slugger was happy and easygoing; he responded calmly to changes in his environment, other dogs, strangers, and even loud or unusual noises. The little Lab loved being with people, yet he was neither too clingy nor too independent. His sturdy conformation as well as a health screening on the dogs in his genetic lines helped to ensure Slugger would be robust enough for service work. His playfulness and eagerness to please also helped Sylvia gauge his trainability. The puppy would happily retrieve sticks, toys, socks, anything he could get his mouth around! This hallmark of his Labrador genes would prove vital to his future career.

Recognizing Slugger's potential, Sylvia made room for him in her home and in her heart. She built a strong relationship with the pup and socialized him with other people and dogs. All the while, Sylvia helped her special Labrador understand that learning could be *fun*.

She used play to create the focus and attention that would serve as the basis for his training. Positive rewards also helped Slugger learn good manners. Motivated by treats, toys, praise, and pats, he was a quick study. The enthusiastic young dog learned to ask to be let out for toileting. He learned to settle in his dog crate at night, and to take food and toys that belonged to him while leaving what did not.

Sylvia went on to help her canine student master basic obedience. She taught him to walk calmly on a loose leash without forging ahead or lagging behind. Since it didn't come naturally for Slugger to wear the packs that would soon be part of his working uniform, Sylvia also had to introduce those. She began by putting them on him at mealtimes so that the dog would associate the packs with something he loved. Before long, all she had to say was, "Slugger, time to get dressed," and the Lab would race up to her.

For a year Sylvia praised and corrected, played and loved. Then she passed her well-mannered puppy on to a CCC trainer Vickie Polk. That must have been the hard part, the tear-stained, awful, aching part. Yet Sylvia understood that some gifts must change hands in order to change a life.

Vickie guided the year-old Labrador through the next steps of his journey. Armed with expertise and lots of patience, she taught her canine pupil many advanced service tasks. Like most students, Slugger learned progressively, so Vickie used positive rewards to build on the training Sylvia had begun.

Cheese and praise encouraged the Lab to bump elevator buttons with his nose. Practice helped him learn to heel quietly alongside his partner when she walked or used a cane or wheelchair.

Once the puppy learned these and other skills, Vickie raised the criteria so that, gradually, more challenging tasks earned rewards. Then she added variables such as a change in environment, sounds and sights, slowly introducing Slugger to the pressures he would encounter as a service dog.

He had to learn to work calmly and enthusiastically in places where most dogs would never go—shopping malls, restaurants, banks, schools full of inquisitive, bouncy youngsters. Vickie knew such preparation was essential.

She also knew that once the young Labrador mastered his task work and gained maturity and confidence, he would need to continue his journey. She loved Slugger, and like Sylvia before her, Vickie let him go.

Only through that sacrifice could Slugger's path join with mine.

Now, as I hurried to the library, the thought of meeting this special dog made my heart race. My breath came warm and fast; it curled back at me from the heavy glass of the library's front door. I pressed my face up to the pane for a moment, peering into the hallway on the other side. The usually teeming corridor was nearly empty; I imagined many of its patrons relished the chance to spend this beautiful day outdoors. But I was here to meet Vickie and Slugger, so I was thrilled.

I stepped inside. Suddenly I was too excited to move or even think clearly. I stood motionless in the doorway while a single realization filled my whole being: *I was going to meet Slugger!*

I couldn't tell how much time passed before a noise, soft yet insistent, pulled me from my trance. A woman was standing outside, tapping lightly on the door. She was grinning, wearing a Caring Canine Companions T-shirt and holding a leash loosely in her left hand. The dog on the other end of the leash was beautiful and powerfully built.

His coat was yellow, sprinkled with white. It was the color of sunshine. A green pack was fastened across the dog's back, yet he didn't seem to be concerned with it. He stood calmly beside his trainer. Only his tail waved as he gazed at me with huge, brown eyes.

Looking back at him, I decided this was the most incredible animal I'd ever seen. I would have been happy simply watching him for hours. Then it struck me, *For goodness sake, move out of the way so they can come in!*

The pair stepped neatly into the room, and the woman turned to me. "Are you Leigh?"

"Yeah," I answered through a grin that nearly reached my ears.

"Great! I'm Vickie, and this fellow here is Slugger." She gave the dog's head a quick pat.

Vickie and I filled our introductions with friendly questions and laughter. I tried to look her in the eye as we talked, but my gaze kept drifting downward. I couldn't stop staring at Slugger. He seemed to share my curiosity; he eventually stretched toward me, plastered his wet nose against my knee, and inhaled. I giggled at his snuffled greeting.

I longed to reach down and stroke Slugger's head, to feel the softness of his fur. But Sylvia had told me that petting a service dog when it was dressed in its packs would disrupt its training, so I jammed my hands into my jeans pocket to resist the temptation.

When Vickie asked Slugger, "What do you say, boy? Are you ready to show Leigh what you can do?" I chimed in, as eager as a kid on Christmas morning.

"Please!" We headed to a vacant conference room at the far end of the library. I scampered to one of the puffy office chairs there and plopped down.

"We'll show you some of the basics first," Vickie said, smiling at me. "Just watch and listen for now."

She had Slugger demonstrate obedience tasks. Then she told me that many service dogs are trained to bark on command. "Slugger can work a bit like a personal safety system for you," she explained. "For example, if you fall and need another person's help, the dog will bark to alert others that something is wrong. All you have to do is this."

Vickie turned her attention to the Labrador and commanded, "Slugger, bark." Obediently, the dog let out a single hearty *Woof!* I was both startled and awed by the deep, booming sound, and Vickie was pleased. "Good boy!" she said, patting the top of the dog's head.

Next she walked Slugger across the room to where a light switch was affixed to the wall. She tapped its metal plate, "Slugger, light!" Following her enthusiastic command, the Lab stood up on his hind legs. He fit his mouth around the switch and nudged it downward until the light clicked off.

I could barely believe what I'd just seen. I sat in the darkened room too stunned to speak. There was a gleam in the trainer's eye when she said, "It's important for service dogs to provide assistance in public and in the home. Slugger's ability to turn lights on and off would be helpful if you were too tired or ill to get them yourself, or if you were ever seated in a wheelchair. Watch this."

Now she repeated the "light" command and pointed to the fixture. Slugger dashed over to it, hopped up, and used his mouth to switch the light on before returning to Vickie's side.

Now my speechless haze dissolved with a single word. "Amazing!"

A cloth pouch was fastened around Vickie's waist; she shoved the fingers of her right hand into it and extracted a small, bright orange cube—cheese.

"Slugger's favorite reward," she informed me as she offered it to him.

The Labrador gulped the treat with such fervor that I proclaimed, "Supersonic gusto!"

Vickie laughed. "Oh yeah!"

Suddenly in awe of both the dog and his trainer, I asked, "How the heck did you teach him all these things?"

"Three Ps: patience, practice, and positive rewards." Then Vickie grinned. "You know, I think it's time for you to give it a try."

"Huh?" I blinked at her.

"How 'bout taking a short walk with Slugger? Just down to the end of the hallway and back."

I sprang out of my chair so fast that I nearly took

a nosedive. "Sure!"

Vickie led us into the hall. She put a handful of cheese morsels in my right hand and slipped Slugger's leash into my left. "Just walk the way you always do, at your normal pace," she told me. "Try to hold the leash loosely without pulling on it. Tell Slugger to heel. If he starts walking faster than you, just stop. Stand still and say 'heel' again. When he walks nicely at your side, praise him and give him a treat. That's all there is to it. This will help you see what it's like to work together. I'll wait right here for you. Got it?"

"Got it," I said, though I wasn't at all sure I did. I breathed deeply, looked down at the yellow Labrador. "Slugger, heel," I said. With that, we took our first steps together. The dog was accustomed to working with Vickie, and his claws sent a brisk *tap-tap, tap-tap* down the corridor. My own movements were slow and tedious. Before we'd traveled more than a few steps, Slugger had pulled ahead of me.

Remembering Vickie's instructions, I stopped. I stood still and re-stated the command, "Slugger, heel." To my astonishment he backed up and positioned himself correctly beside me.

"Good boy!" I exclaimed. I offered him a piece of cheese, and we continued our walk. Each time the dog moved ahead of me, I stopped, repeated the heel command, and started once more. The process seemed painstakingly slow. By the time I'd uttered my fifth heel command, I was beginning to wonder if this powerful, brilliant dog would ever actually adjust to my wobbly-legged gait.

But then it happened. We resumed our walk, and

this time, *this* time Slugger didn't rush forward. He moved beside me, glancing up repeatedly as if trying to gauge my unfamiliar stride. His steps were cautious; his pace matched my own. I was amazed. For so long, keeping up with others had been my definition of grace.

When I was a child, that grace often deserted me, vanishing like mist in sunlight. I recalled one particular afternoon in fourth grade. I was on the playground with my classmates, standing in a relay line. I stared down at my shoes. Their scuffed toes reminded me of things I wanted to forget: *Not today*, I'd vowed. *I'm not going to fall this time.*

The line moved steadily forward as runners took off one after another. My classmates cheered. They jumped around, and thumped the shoulders of the fastest racers, "Good job! Good job, man!" Our team was ahead.

I yelled at the red-faced boy who suddenly charged toward me, "Way to go! Run!" I inhaled, held out my hand. He slapped it with a sweaty palm as he crossed the line. My turn.

Oh God! I willed my body into a frantic trot. My mind took up a chant: *Left. Right. Keep going. Left. Right. Don't fall. Left. Right. It's easy.* Then I heard the soft crunch of my opponent's sneakers in the dirt. Her ponytail bobbed up and down as she ran past me. My teammates screamed, "No!"

The voice inside me screamed louder; *Keep up, you stupid feet, for once in your life run fast!"*

I tried to pick up speed, and my left foot slammed against the uneven earth. My ankle gave in. I stumbled forward, fighting to regain some balance. Then I crashed. The rough ground tore my skin. I felt blood trickling down my right leg, and dripping from a gash on my cheek. Droplets splattered like scarlet paint in the dirt.

In fourth grade I knew the only thing worse than falling in front of my classmates was letting them see me cry, so I swallowed hard against the sobs rising in my throat. The yelling that had filled the air was gone, replaced by whispering and pointing. One of the fastest runners on our team, Jimmy, snorted loudly and spat.

He shoved his fingers through his sweaty hair. "Why do we got to have a hop-along on our team? She's nothing but a *cripple*; she can't even run. She's so weird, man!" Such taunts echoed through my childhood.

Today the sneers were silenced. With Slugger, there was no race to be won; there was only a path to be traveled together. Suddenly I was filled with the urge to interrupt our sojourn, to bend down and hug the Labrador. Still, I imagined that wasn't part of appropriate service dog protocol.

Instead I practically sang, "Good boy, Slugger! What great heeling, you smart, gorgeous animal!" I gave him an extra big piece of cheese. The dog's body swayed lightly against my leg, following the rhythm of his wagging tail.

When we turned and retraced our steps down the hall to where Vickie was waiting, Slugger and I moved slowly, awkwardly; but we moved *together*. After a lifetime of struggling to keep up with others, I found myself accompanied by an incredible dog, one willing to walk beside me at my pace.

Inspired, I whispered to him. "I know I've got a funky hustle, boy. But I'll bet we could find our own rhythm if you're up for it." For now there was simply the measured tread of foot and paw. And the hopeful pounding of my heart.

"Slugger's the neatest dog in the world!" Forgetting good library manners, I broadcast my reviews loudly down the hall before we had even reached Vickie. By the time the Labrador and I were at her side, I couldn't stop talking. "He did a great job for me! Didn't you, boy?"

Two morsels of cheese remained in my hand. They were squishy-soft around the edges now, but Slugger gobbled them happily. He wagged his tail and licked his jowls. Then he burped. "Is that his way of saying thanks?" I grinned at Vickie.

She didn't return my smile. Tears made wet, serpentine tracks down her face. Suddenly I felt as if my heart had plunged into my stomach. "Oh! What's wrong?"

"Nothing's wrong," Vickie answered. "That's just it; it's *right*." She brushed a tear from her cheek and continued, "I know this dog, and when I see how he responds to you, there's no doubt in my mind. You two are destined to be a team. That's more than my hunch. It's something Slugger knows."

Chapter 4

First Lessons

In the days that followed, I discovered just how *much* Slugger knew. It had taken nearly two years for him to complete his training and prepare for our partnership. Now it was my turn. Slugger's training was founded on practice, patience, and positive rewards—what Vickie called the three Ps—and I realized that my side of the deal would hinge, at least initially, on the three Cs: confidence, consistency, and lots and lots of cheese.

Though I'd once considered blocks of cheddar, Swiss, and American cheese mundane, I quickly found myself swept up in the Labrador's cheese-centric passion. While Slugger's devotion was driven by his taste buds, my newfound fondness was based on something other than flavor. As the dog's preferred reward, cheese was powerful stuff. So I made sure to have a huge supply of it for my first partner-training session.

CCC's training facility was located an hour and a half from my home, and when I arrived at the white brick building, Vickie and Slugger greeted me at the door. "Well, hi there!" Slugger's trainer welcomed me. "Come on in." Slugger, I noticed, wasn't wearing his packs, and as I stepped inside, all I could think of was petting him.

Vickie ushered me into a large, brightly lit room with a concrete floor. "Hang onto him a minute, and I'll grab a chair for you." She handed me Slugger's green nylon leash. "Slugger, stay." He looked from Vickie to me, then back to Vickie. When his trainer scurried to the far side of the building, only his eyes followed her.

My own eyes were fixed on the Labrador. I reached down and petted him. Slugger was two and a half years old, but his coat was still thick and downy, like new puppy fur. I buried my fingertips in its softness. Smitten, I stroked his back and crooned, "Your fur is like silken sunshine!"

The dog looked up at me and wagged. Then he turned his gaze back to his trainer. When she approached, carrying a lawn chair under one arm and Slugger's packs in the other, his tail waved faster.

"Here you go," Vickie said, setting the chair next to me. She thumped Slugger's sides playfully. "Good stay, boy." Reluctantly, I handed her his leash.

"Now the very first thing you need to know when working with a service dog is that he's a dog," Vickie began.

I'd been nervous about this first training session, worried I might be overwhelmed, but so far things were off to a smooth start. A service dog is a dog. I could handle that.

"Don't expect Slugger to act like a little person in a fluffy jacket, because that's not what he is," Vickie continued. "He's not a machine, either, so you can't just press a button or turn a dial to get him to do what you want. Like you, your dog will have good days and bad. You'll both mess up sometimes—even after you've been together for years. But the goal here isn't perfection; it's teamwork. That's what I'll try to teach you."

I realized then that Vickie's seemingly obvious statement—a service dog is a dog—wasn't as simple as I'd first believed. I had lots to learn.

"Think of Slugger as having two modes," his trainer said, "the work mode—that's when he's in his packs and helping you, and the non-work mode—when he's just hanging out being a regular dog. Slugger knows the difference. I'll show you."

The Lab—in regular dog mode—had been meandering around us sniffing the floor while Vickie talked. When called, he came to stand in front of his trainer. He was wagging and wiggling so mightily that his whole back end swayed. Vickie scratched behind his ear. Then she said, "Okay, big guy, time to get dressed. Slugger, stand."

The dog's wiggles disappeared; Vickie's words seemed to smooth them like a warm iron on a crinkled shirt. Slugger stood perfectly still as his trainer put the green pack onto his back and fastened two large buckles underneath. Once dressed, he became so focused on Vickie that even the wag of his tail changed. It waved with a slow and steady swing I would later dub his "working wag."

"See? When he's in work mode, Slugger should be tuned in," Vickie said. "He must deal with distractions—people, loud noises, other animals, a scrap of food on the ground—all without losing his focus on his partner."

I thought about how easily my own brain was often sidetracked, "Wow, that's one heck of a work ethic!"

Vickie smiled. "Sure is! It's also something you'll have to enforce when the two of you become partners."

Just the idea of being partnered with the incredible Labrador inspired me. Near the end of our first training session, I made a vow: I'd do whatever it took to learn to work with him the way his trainer did. Together Vickie and Slugger moved with the ease and grace of dancers. *They make it look seamless!* I thought as I watched them.

I soon discovered that such seamless teamwork was in fact a carefully considered series of steps. These were the steps I would need to master, so I made a mental note of every single thing Vickie did. She executed even the most basic commands with precision. If she wanted Slugger to sit, Vickie began by calling his name.

The moment she had the dog's undivided attention, his trainer said, "Sit." When Slugger obediently dropped his hind end to the floor, Vickie exclaimed, "Good boy!" Her praise was immediately followed by a small bite of cheese. Slugger's tail swished furiously as he gulped it. Clearly this was his favorite part of the exercise. Vickie assured me it was also an important part of team communication.

I tried to hold on to all the wisdom she shared. Still, doubt often pulled at the edges of my concentration. It whispered, soft and insidious, *You can't even control your own body. What makes you think this remarkable animal will listen to you?*

The answer to that question eluded me as Vickie passed me the dog's leash during a training session a few days later. Now it was my turn to make Slugger sit. The leather lead slid in my sweaty hand. My throat tightened. The voice in my mind hissed, *That dog isn't going to obey you.*

I plunged ahead anyway. Looking down at the big Lab, I said, "Slugger sit?" My voice came out squeaky and wheedling, like that of an annoying cartoon character.

The dog didn't even twitch. He just stood there. *Now what?* I glanced at Vickie and lifted my eyebrows.

"Try that again," she said, "and this time tell him what you want, instead of asking him."

Don't ask, tell. I took a deep breath and pushed the words through my lips once more. "Slugger, sit." It was a command now.

The Labrador's butt promptly dropped to the floor.

"Good dog!" My praise was followed by a cheddar reward. I was proud of Slugger and of myself, too.

"Nice job," Vickie congratulated me. "You know, Slugger just taught you a lesson. When you want him to do something, say it like you mean it. If you get all wishy-washy, he'll pick up on that. If you're confident, your dog will be, too."

As a child, I was never sure of myself; instead I'd been convinced of my own weirdness. I'd been told that because of my disability I had to be not only tough, but also better than other people. This, I'd believed, was my redemption, a chance to make amends for my weirdness.

When I was little, I was a dynamo of compensation. I made straight A's. I made jokes. I earned a reputation as one of the best-behaved kids in my school. *See?* the voice inside me demanded then, *I may be crippled, but I am smarter, funnier, nicer than others.* I'd always prayed that would be enough.

Now I let out a quick, sharp laugh and confessed, "I guess confidence has never been my strong suit."

"Don't worry," Vickie answered gently. "All of this takes time. But hang in there. It will come, I promise."

Slowly, very slowly, that promise proved true. With help from both Vickie and Sylvia, Slugger and I honed our team skills. Sylvia took us to visit her friend Mr. Martin, a kind, soft-spoken man who fashioned the leather equipment for the horses in his Amish community.

After carefully measuring both Slugger and me, he crafted a support harness for us. Its padded leather straps fit snuggly across Slugger's chest, and a firm handle extended up from the dog's haunches so that I could hold on to it as we walked. Using this custom-made gear we practiced basic obedience, proper heeling, and task work over and over.

The repetition taught me to keep my interactions

with Slugger consistent. When I gave commands uniformly and held to steady expectations, the dog's responses became dependable as well. Each small success built my confidence and strengthened my bond with my new canine partner. Still, there was no doubt about it: teamwork was *hard* work!

Vickie understood this, and one day after a particularly demanding training session, she suggested, "Why don't you plan to come out to my house for our next meeting? We'll just relax, go over a few things, and let the dogs play." Slugger's trainer lived on a small farm with her husband, an assortment of dogs, two cats, several horses, and a little flock of chickens. A visit there sounded perfect.

Days later I pulled into her driveway and was greeted by the canine pack. Slugger, in regular dog mode, was the first to reach me. Close on his heels was his best four-footed buddy, a tiny Yorkie named Chris. White-coated Nikki dashed up next. Then Princess, the German shepherd—whom Vickie had told me ruled the place—made her magnificent appearance.

I greeted each dog in turn, circling back instinctively to give Slugger extra pats and ear scratches. Though I hadn't uttered any commands, the Labrador took up perfect heel position beside me as I walked to the house. I imagined this was his way of telling his pack mates, "She's with me!"

By the time I was settled in Vickie's comfortable living room with a glass of iced tea I felt right at home. Slugger's trainer regaled me with hilarious stories of her animals' antics. A cat stretched languidly across the sofa back and blinked its amber eyes.

The dogs ambled through the house, stopping frequently to collect pats as they passed through the living room. But Slugger soon upped his bids for my attention. He approached me with a half-flattened, grubby soccer ball and deposited it in my lap.

Vickie chuckled. "That's his favorite toy, you know."

I'd pretty much guessed that from the ball's condition, so I rumpled the top of the Lab's head and told him I thought the gross and stinky thing was a treasure. Encouraged, he proceeded to bring me a scrappy, stuffed mouse whose ears had been gnawed off, a plastic bone, and a grass stained tennis shoe.

"He sure is showing off for you; I swear, even my garden shoe!" Vickie grabbed the latest offering and tossed it lightly into the corner. "Speaking of the garden, you want to see the rest of the place?"

I'd been hoping she'd offer; when we reached the barn where the air smelled sweet and earthy and horses poked their heads from their stalls to whinny softly at us, I figured this was the best spot on the tour. Slugger didn't seem to agree.

He'd been doing a stunning impersonation of an old farm hound, sniffing along the rows of squash and peas in the garden, eyeing the pen where chickens clucked and scratched at the earth, and tromping through the tall grass at the fence line like he owned the place. But as soon as we stepped inside the barn, he high-tailed it toward the half open door at the far side of the building.

I'd never seen him move so fast. "What the . . . ?"

I gasped.

"Shit!" Vickie yelled. She took off after the yellow blur that was Slugger.

It wasn't until she returned, moments later, hanging onto the dog's collar and fussing, that I realized Vickie's exclamation had been quite literal: she'd just barely managed to keep Slugger from diving headlong into the manure pile outside. "Oh yeah," she said, wiping the sweat from her face and panting nearly as hard as the Lab, "Did I mention Slugger likes to roll in horse crap?"

Those words stayed in my mind. For days after my visit to the farm I had only to remember them and I would start giggling. Still, they drove home one of the most important lessons Vickie had shared during our very first training session: A service dog is a dog.

Chapter 5

The Path to Partnership

"You up for some pizza?" I had just arrived for another session of training, and Vickie's question caught me off guard.

"Um, sure," I stammered. "I reckon there's no bad time for pizza. Why?"

"I got a two-for-one coupon for the buffet at the little Italian place downtown Harrisonburg." Vickie opened the passenger door of her blue Dodge Ram. "Come on, I'm starved," she said as she helped me scramble in.

"Where's . . . ?" before I'd finished my question, Slugger popped his head through the truck cab's open window. He sniffed my ear and licked the side of my face.

"Hey, you!" I looped an arm around his neck, planting a kiss on his velvet muzzle.

"Look at you two, acting like you've been together for years. I'd say you're ready for your first lunch date. Hope you don't mind me tagging along," Vickie teased. It hit me then; I was going out to a restaurant with my service dog!

Slugger had visited many restaurants while in training. He didn't even twitch a whisker as we stepped into the pizza parlor. But I was grinning nonstop, nearly bouncing over the plaid-carpeted floor. With the Labrador at my side and his trainer following, I wove carefully through the crowded room, feeling as if I'd been granted instant celebrity.

A little girl warbled "Look, a doggie!" She leaned from her chair and wiggled a greasy-fingered greeting in Slugger's direction. "You gonna eat some pizza? Good doggie!" Slugger's admirer was too young to understand that assistance animals are never fed from the table. Still, she was perceptive; she knew a good dog when she saw one.

Vickie and I headed toward an empty booth near the buffet. Slugger was at my side. I'd learned to interpret the feel of his leash in my hand. Its position and tension communicated almost as clearly as spoken words. A sudden tug—something was out of synch.

Quickly I scanned my surroundings to locate the distraction. *There!* Perched nearby on the green and red checked rug was a meatball. Now Slugger gazed at it with an expression so full of longing that I imagined him composing verses like a lovelorn poet. *Ah, darling meatball, I do crave your flavor; but sadly, your spices I shall never savor! Most wonderful morsel, if only I could . . .*

"Slugger, leave it," I ordered, refocusing my thoughts and directing my dog. The Labrador huffed softly. He walked past the minced meat temptation and lay down on the floor beneath our booth.

"Nice job," Vickie said. "Now tell him to stay put, and let's go get some lunch!"

The aroma of Italian food, piquant and enticing, made my mouth water; still I felt nervous about leaving Slugger. We'd practiced stays so many times during training. *Will all that practice hold up now?* I wondered. *Will Slugger listen to me or will he decide to make a break for it and go after the fallen meatball?* I swallowed my uncertainties and summoned my sternest voice to give the command, "Slugger, stay."

Tail wag.

"Think you can take that as a 'Yes, ma'am,'" Vickie laughed. I followed her to the buffet. Piling breadsticks and pizza slices onto a warm, white plate, I couldn't help wondering if the dog was maintaining his stay. Quickly I peeked back over my shoulder.

The sight nearly made me spill my food. Slugger was beneath our booth exactly where I'd left him; and he was watching me, staring so intently it was as if his hazel eyes were absorbing me.

His tail drummed a welcome against the floor when I returned. I smiled and settled into the puffy green vinyl of the booth. I'd just begun to tuck into my Italian feast when a sudden heaviness overtook my left foot. I was used to the dead weight of exhaustion in my body, but this feeling was different. It was warm. A red cloth covered our table, draping down the sides like a stage curtain; the fringe sewn around its edge tickled my hand as I shoved it back to get a glimpse of my leaden appendage. "What the . . . ?"

Slugger lifted his ears slightly at my exclamation. The rest of his head remained still. It rested completely—and apparently comfortably—atop my foot. The Labrador met my gaze then. The sweetness of his expression made my breath catch. In that moment I realized: the purest devotion can pass from one heart to another without a sound.

After the success of our "first working lunch," Slugger and I began visiting familiar places like the grocery store, the bank, and the campus of JMU, where I'd be returning in the fall to complete my master's degree. These public outings marked the progress of our partnership.

Though I still felt flashes of trepidation from time to time, new and positive feelings began to take root within me. Slugger's presence by my side brought me dynamic confidence; what started as belief in my dog gradually grew into trust of our partnership. Acknowledging my own role and value in that partnership enabled me to take my first tentative steps toward real self-assurance.

I needed every ounce of that confidence on the bright afternoon when Vickie announced that a professional pet photographer was holding a shoot in a local pet shop and it was time for Slugger and me to get our team picture done. I knew this place would hold lots of distractions for my dog, so as I stepped into the loud and bustling store, I used my firmest voice, "Slugger, heel."

He looked up at me with an expression that read, "You got it, boss!"

The two of us moved easily among the displays at the front of the store. When I paused to admire a denim shirt with the head of a yellow Lab embroidered on the lapel, Vickie called, "Looks like Slugger, doesn't it?" She was following a few paces behind us so she could observe our teamwork and offer pointers.

I glanced back at her and grinned. Over the past few weeks, I'd developed an obsession for all things Labrador. "Yeah, I might just buy it!"

"Good idea, but you should probably get in line for the photos first, before it gets crowded." Vickie motioned toward the back of the store where a cluster of pets and their people had begun to congregate.

Nodding, I threaded my way down an aisle stocked with bird supplies. Slugger pranced along beside me, completely unconcerned with the shelves full of toys, feed, and cages. He even skirted around a pile of birdseed that had spilled onto the floor, lifting his paws high as if he couldn't stand the idea of stepping in the stuff while he was on the job. I grinned as I watched him.

I was so preoccupied with Slugger's seed-avoidance dance that we'd made it part way down the next aisle before I recognized where we were. Lo and behold, I was now steering us right through the middle of the dog treats!

Oh damn, I should have been looking where I was going, the voice in my head fussed. The pungent aromas of pigs' ears, and liver bites, yogurt drops, and cheese snacks filled my Lab's nose. His nostrils twitched and flared. He turned his head first to one side and then the other, following the siren scents.

I could almost feel the quiver of temptation coursing through his body, up the leash, and into my own hand. Though we'd successfully practiced lots of 'distraction work' in training, this time I couldn't think straight, couldn't figure out what to do. Flustered, I froze.

"Remember, you've got to keep moving and give your dog some direction," Vickie's voice cut through the confusion in my brain.

Right! Pushing my wobbly legs into motion once more, I talked to Slugger, "Let's go, boy, heel!" This seemed to do the trick. I breathed a sigh of relief as he moved appropriately beside me once more. My solace, however, was short-lived. Orange, rawhide chips waited at the end of the aisle. Not only were the cheddar-flavored chews loose in a bin, they were also right at Slugger's level. My cheese-loving dog charged toward them, licking his chops.

Disapproval snapped in my words then. "Slugger, no pull!"

My partner's perked ears dropped. I imagined his mind wired like a television, my steely command flipping its channel from the Cheese Broadcasting Station back to Team Now Network. He stopped tugging and took up heel position.

"Good dog!"

We joined the pets and people waiting at the photographer's booth. A pair of lop-eared rabbits peered at us from behind their wire cage, and a fuzzy, white pup barely bigger than Slugger's paw lunged on the end of its bejeweled leash.

But my dog, apparently unwilling to let his work mode slide again, ignored them. I praised him and offered a big chunk of cheese. Slugger's eyes glazed over with unabashed desire. He slurped his reward from my palm, leaving a huge glob of drool in its place. Without thinking, I wiped my hand on my thigh.

It wasn't until I was seated in front of the camera a few minutes later that it hit me; my first service dog team picture would feature me, my gorgeous partner, and a slimy trail of dog spit on my leg.

I could only smile at my canine companion as the camera clicked. I knew our path to partnership wouldn't always be smooth, and it might—I now realized—be slicked with slobber.

If Slugger had his way, that path would also include even more corporeal elements. This was evident on the day I joined Vickie for my first public presentation.

A local civic group had invited her to give a talk about service dogs. Such engagements were great for raising funds as well as awareness, and though I wasn't comfortable speaking yet, I was happy to accompany Vickie. Since my team instruction with Slugger was nearing its end, she had begun to train a new pup, a charming black Lab named Zack. She loaded both canine pupils into her truck and met me in town just before our scheduled appearance.

Dressed in my official, pink *Caring Canine Companions* shirt, I hopped from my car and waved as Vickie pulled her big blue truck into the parking lot of the church that would host our presentation. I noticed my usually easygoing friend seemed ruffled.

She scrambled out of her truck and hurried around to the back, where the dogs were waiting to be let out. Giving Zack a firm order to stay, Vickie unloaded Slugger and handed me his leash. She smiled, then rolled her eyes. "He's *your* dog today, Leigh!"

"Hey there," I said, running my fingers over the top of the Labrador's head.

"I'd be careful where you pet that rascal, and don't sniff him too close," his trainer advised. "You know he loves the manure pile. I did my best, but I think his right ear's still green."

Remembering Slugger's mad dash to the far end of the horse barn on the afternoon of my visit, I gasped.

"I spent so much time bathing and grooming both dogs this morning, and wouldn't you know it?" Vickie shook her head as if she still couldn't believe what had taken place. "Slugger snuck out of the house and took a romp in the pile!" I only had time to wipe him off before we came."

I looped an arm over Vickie's shoulder. "Sure makes for a rough start to the day."

"Yeah, for me, but not for Slugger. He thought

the whole thing was great!" She chuckled.

I looked down at the dog. His eyes sparkled. His tail waved jauntily through the air. The smudges that streaked his neck and right ear like earth-toned graffiti didn't seem to bother him one bit.

Vickie gave Slugger a quick pat before unloading Zack. Then she grinned at me. "I reckon we should go on inside. Zack and I will lead the way. You and your smelly, green-eared dog can bring up the rear."

Giggling, I followed her to the building's cool basement. Several dozen folks awaited us there. A woman in a plaid skirt and crisp white blouse ushered us warmly to the front of the room.

She addressed her colleagues, "Okay, everyone, we'd like to get started. We're honored to have with us Vickie Polk and Leigh Brill from Caring Canine Companions of Virginia. They're going to be telling us a little bit about their lovely dogs." She turned and smiled at the Labradors who were now lying quietly in heel position. "How beautiful! And so calm, too!"

Sensing appreciation in the woman's tone, Slugger flicked his tail twice. "Well you're welcome, gorgeous!" His admirer cooed. Laughter rippled through the audience as she settled into to an empty folding chair.

Now Vickie stood. "Thank you all for inviting us. I'm a trainer with Caring Canine Companions. This is Zack, my newest student."

She gestured to the black Lab. Then she pointed toward me. "That's Leigh and her new service dog, Slugger. They've joined us today, so Leigh can see what it's like to be on this side of a presentation. The two of them have been working really hard finishing up their team training, and I'm happy to say they're turning into an impressive pair. Slugger does a great job helping Leigh deal with the challenges of her cerebral palsy."

Vickie paused and beamed at me, but I was suddenly besieged by a wave of panic. *Oh God*, the voice in my head shrieked, *I can't believe she just told a room full of strangers I have CP!* Now I was afraid to look at the audience, afraid I'd find their faces pinched by morbid curiosity. I'd encountered such expressions all my life.

My CP was the great secret of my childhood. It was only spoken of when I was admitted to the nearby medical center for multiple surgeries and post-op treatment.

There, my secret became a label—one that identified and defined me. Every time I passed through the hospital's heavy doors I felt my normal kid self fall away.

I became a case to be observed, managed, and ultimately fixed. White-coated medical students peered at my sleeping body even before I woke up in the mornings. They followed me around all day, discussing me the same way gawking zoo-goers talk about snakes or chimpanzees.

One afternoon when I was eight years old, I

showed up for a physical therapy session and discovered a flock of medical students waiting there. They were scattered throughout the therapy room, but the moment my therapist, Andie, helped me onto a floor mat, they circled round me.

Andie told me she had to take a phone call in her office. "While I'm gone," she said, "you can get started with your hamstring stretches. Those aren't too hard; you should be fine until I get back. These guys will keep you company in the meantime." She gestured to the students, but when she disappeared, they just stood above me and whispered to each other. I couldn't make out what they were saying. They held cameras.

I decided this might be a good time for me to say something funny, like, "Ooh, what nice shins you have!" But I suddenly felt too nervous to be witty. I began my stretches.

A female student tapped the edge of the therapy mat with the toe of her stylish boot. "This is a CP case, right?"

Her voice was shrill and choppy, like the bawking of a chicken. From my spot on the floor I looked up and noticed her nose. It was long and pointy, beaklike. I silently dubbed this woman Chickenhead. I wished I had the guts to say, "Hey, Chickenhead, I'm a kid, not a case!"

I was still trying to find the nerve to say that, when Chickenhead squatted down. "I need a picture of that." She pointed her camera at my hips. Clicked. I forced myself to ignore her and concentrate on my stretches.

Next, a bearded student leaned down. He was so close I got a nose-full of his cologne. "I've got to get this," he said. He scrunched up his face, aimed his camera. Four clicks and he moved away.

The others followed suit. One by one they leaned in and took pictures of my body. They didn't tell me why they wanted those pictures. They didn't ask me if they could take them. They didn't even *talk* to me. Instead, they talked among themselves. A man with an olive complexion snapped a picture. Then he turned to Chickenhead. "Do you think she knows how bad her body is?"

I wanted to scream at the man then. I wanted to tell him, and Chickenhead, and all of them, "I'm not a freak!" But when I looked up, their scowling faces said otherwise.

As a child I learned to expect such expressions whenever people were told the name of my condition. Now, sitting in the cool church basement, I didn't want to see them again. Blushing fiercely, I stared at the floor.

An unexpected sound made me lift my gaze. It started softly, then erupted like raindrops in a summer shower. Applause. Looking out at the audience, I saw not grimaces but smiles. Tears sprang to my eyes as I realized: These people I didn't even know had just learned the greatest secret and shame of my childhood, my cerebral palsy. And yet they were clapping. They were clapping for me and my dog.

Sensing my emotion, Slugger wiggled closer and nuzzled my foot. Vickie continued with her presentation, but now I was only focused on the truth that whispered over and over in my mind like the lyrics of an old country song. Reaching down to stroke Slugger's fur, I shared that truth with him: I love you, I sure love you, my smelly, green-eared dog!

Chapter 6

The Test

The final step to make my partnership with Slugger official was certification; this meant facing something I dreaded—a test. I'd always been a perfectionist. As a youngster I'd obsessed over every spelling test, math quiz, and science exam of my academic career. Now my mind was consumed by the specifics of team certification.

This test, I knew, was far more important than the pen and paper kind. Designed to ensure that Slugger was stable and well behaved in public, it would also appraise our task performance, and be so challenging that our previous outings would seem like the proverbial walk in the park. Ironically, much of my certification with Slugger was actually set up in a park—a real, public park that just happened to be hosting a regional dog show on the day of our test.

Sylvia had chosen this venue for a reason. If I could handle Slugger amid the sights, sounds, and smells of a busy dog show, she was certain I'd be able to work with him anywhere!

On the morning of the test, Sylvia, Vickie, Slugger, and I met at Hardees for a quick breakfast. Vickie staked out a large booth while Sylvia, bearing the clipboard that held our all-important evaluation forms, followed Slugger and me toward the restaurant's front counter. "I'll help you carry stuff," she said, but I knew CCC's president was also critiquing my work with Slugger.

It seemed my canine partner sensed this too; he heeled perfectly at my side and sat quietly as I placed our order.

I'd gotten as far as two coffees and one large orange juice when the server peered down at my Labrador. He declared, "No dogs allowed in here!"

Crap, I thought, *a confrontation is the last thing I need on test day!* Unaccustomed to standing up for myself, I ran my fingers quickly over the top of Slugger's head to steady my nerves. Thankfully Vickie and Sylvia had taught me what to do if someone said I could not bring Slugger into a public place.

I took a deep breath and uttered what I'd learned. "This is my service dog. He helps me deal with my physical disability, and under the Americans with Disabilities Act, he's legally allowed to accompany me." My words came out sounding far more calm and confident than I felt.

The employee stood silently for a moment. He scratched his head, blinked, and then said simply, "Oh. What else you want?"

He took the rest of my order and scuttled off to fill it by the time I realized that Sylvia had sidled up next to me. "Atta girl!" She punched my arm playfully. "That confrontation wasn't even part of your test, but you handled it like a pro. You're doing great!"

Encouraged by her words and my own success so far, I nearly pranced to our booth. Sylvia carried our food, and I decided to have Slugger carry something as well. I held my red leather wallet in front of him and gave the command, "Slugger, take it." Obediently, he clamped his jaws around the purse. "Hold," I ordered. And he did.

Bam! A sudden loud noise cracked through the air. Instinctively I jumped, but Slugger remained steady at my side. I took a deep breath and scanned the room to find the source of the sound. "Sorry 'bout that, gal," Sylvia said, bending down to retrieve the clipboard she'd just slammed against the floor. "I had to make sure our boy could handle loud, unexpected noises while working—all part of your test."

"Right." I smiled sheepishly. "I just hope our score doesn't depend on *me* staying calm under those conditions!"

"It's okay that you jumped clear out of your skin." Sylvia winked. "I'm just pleased to see that Slugger kept up his concentration. He didn't even drop your purse. Solid work!"

The Labrador's tail waved proudly as he carried my wallet all the way back to our booth. He didn't release it until I reached down and said, "Slugger, give."

"Good job, you two!" Vickie said. I grinned. As I ate my breakfast, I silently prayed that we'd be able to keep it up.

It wasn't long before I found out how that prayer would be answered. The park was teeming with people and dogs when we arrived. My heart raced as Vickie pulled her truck into one of the few empty spots. I slid out of the passenger's seat and scampered around to the back of the vehicle before she'd even had time to unbuckle her seat belt. When she joined me a moment later, she gave me a good-natured nudge. "Ready to get started, huh?"

"Yeah, kinda nervous, too."

"I know y'all will do just fine." Vickie turned to Slugger who was standing on the tailgate waiting to get out. "Won't you, boy?" She rested her hand on his head as if bestowing a blessing, then handed me his leash. "He's all yours!"

Slugger's eyes were bright and alert. His perked ears and twitching nostrils left no doubt that he was taking in as much information as possible from our surroundings. But I couldn't let him out of the truck until Sylvia was with us. She'd parked her car further down the lot and by the time she reached us, she was sweating from her hike in the summer's heat. "All set, gal and dog?" she asked, running a hand across her brow.

"Yep!" I stood for a moment and inhaled deeply. The dog was perfectly still now, waiting.

"Slugger, unload." The instant the command left my lips, he leapt neatly from the truck and took up heel position.

"Okay, let's take a stroll!" Sylvia announced. We made our way through the parking lot, stopping as vehicles passed us. Unfazed by them, Slugger worked calmly at my side. I knew that Sylvia would be noting this, checking off two more key points in our certification: controlled unload from a vehicle and appropriate behavior around traffic.

We headed toward a tree-lined sidewalk, drawn by the promise of shade. Reaching the curb, I stopped. "Slugger, up."

Slugger didn't move; he just stood there looking at me. The voice in my mind screeched, *Crap, he didn't listen! You messed up. You can kiss your perfect score on this test good-bye now!"* But then I recalled Vickie's words— how she'd said that teamwork is more important than flawlessness. Now I grasped his leash firmly and repeated my command "Slugger, up!" This time my partner placed his front paws on the curb.

"That's it! Good boy!" I grasped the handle of his harness for support. Slugger braced me as I stepped carefully onto the sidewalk. He remained completely still until I'd made it safely over the curb and uttered a cheerful, "Okay!" Then he moved into heel position once more.

"Right then," Sylvia said, "How 'bout we take advantage of the shade here to do your 'sits and downs?'"

Slugger and I had practiced those countless times over the course of our training. People and other dogs were coming and going all around us now, but confidence rang in my voice when I told Slugger to 'Sit.' The dog's hind end dropped to the pavement immediately.

"Very nice," Sylvia said. She walked up and stood directly behind him. From there she did a stunning impersonation of a loquacious, dog-crazy stranger. "Ooooh, what a beeeeautiful animal. How are you today, gorgeous? Huh? Are you doing good today? You're just so pretty I could take you home!"

I giggled at Sylvia's parody. I knew Slugger would have loved to hop up and plant a big, sloppy kiss on her nose, but my well-mannered companion stayed seated while Sylvia tempted him.

He remembered his training even as she circled close, squeaking and cooing. Only the tip of Slugger's tail swished in a sedate acknowledgment. I would come to call that attitude his "econo-wag."

"Hah!" Sylvia guffawed as she moved away. "No breaking the boy's focus today!" She motioned to me. "Now you come over here, and we'll do the six-foot recall."

"Yes ma'am." I suddenly wanted to be as obedient as my dog. Giving him firm orders to down and stay, I scampered over to Sylvia.

Slugger watched me with the same bright-eyed intensity I'd discovered during our first lunch date. I imagined his muscles, like tightly coiled springs, ready to release the moment I called.

The five minutes I had to wait felt like an eternity; still, this was part of our certification—we had to prove that Slugger would stay put regardless of distractions, time, or distance. When Sylvia finally gave me the okay to summon him, he dashed to my side.

He sat and stared up at me with a sweet, expectant expression. I wondered if it meant, *I thought you'd never call!* Or perhaps, *Here I am! Didn't I do well?*

Though there was no way to know the thoughts percolating in Slugger's brain, he had indeed performed this task beautifully. I offered him a chunk of cheese and bent down to give him a hug.

Vickie, meanwhile, was chatting with a woman who was holding a little boy's hand. I had a hunch Slugger's trainer was arranging the next part of our test, so I told my dog to lie down as the trio walked over.

"Hey, Leigh, this is Lynn and her son, Adam." Vickie introduced the pair and patted the youngster's shoulder. "They've agreed to lend a hand for the next part of your certification with Slugger."

Vickie had explained to them that petting a service dog was generally discouraged, but that for our test we needed to demonstrate that Slugger would be friendly and gentle when approached by children too young to understand that.

"We have two Labs at home," Lynn said. "Jake and Emma aren't show dogs or working dogs like yours, but they're part of our family." She squatted down to be at eye level with her son. "Adam, would you like to meet Slugger? He's a very nice and special dog!"

The child gave a wide-eyed nod.

"I'm sure Slugger would love that!" I encouraged. Adam answered with a quick, shy smile, and then bounced his chubby little hand gently on top of Slugger's head.

The dog shifted his position to get a better view of his new friend. Inspired, Adam looped his arms around Slugger's neck and squeezed. Even with this impromptu hug, my service dog maintained his down. Only his tail conveyed his response—it beat joyfully against the pavement.

If I'd ever wondered whether canine happiness was contagious, this moment would have erased all doubt; Adam giggled, his mother beamed, and I suddenly wished I had a tail so I could wag along with my partner. "There's nothing like a good Lab!" Lynn exclaimed, taking her son's hand once more.

I grinned. "You've got that right! And thanks for helping with this part of our certification."

"Our pleasure. Good luck with the rest of it!"

As Lynn and Adam continued their stroll, Vickie whispered in my ear, "You don't need luck; you've got each other!"

My team of two suited me perfectly, but it soon became clear that some of the other dogs around us were anxious to join in and expand our pack. A cute basset hound seemed especially keen on getting to know Slugger. Enjoying some freedom on a long leash, the dog toddled up to him with its nose twitching and its little, white-tipped whip of a tail wagging furiously.

"Lilly," called the man holding the other end of the leash, "have you found a beau already?" But the dog was so enamored with Slugger that she paid her owner no mind. She just kept sniffing and wagging and frisking around on her stubby little legs. And my dog? Perhaps he was drawn to Lilly's long, silky ears. Maybe he caught the twinkle in her soulful eyes.

For the first time all day, Slugger decided to take an unannounced work break. He pulled toward the bouncing basset, momentarily forgetting that he was supposed to be concentrating on me.

"Better give him a correction for that," Sylvia advised, echoing the thought that was blaring in my brain. Instinctively I yanked the dog's leash and ordered, "Slugger, leave it!" Then I called to Lilly's owner, "Please come and get your dog! My service dog is working. He can't play right now."

"Oh God, I didn't realize!" The man ran up, scooped his protesting hound into his arms, and hurried away, leaving a stream of rapid-fire apologies in his wake.

Slugger had now resumed work mode, but I slapped my hand to my face and cringed. "Sure messed that up, didn't I?"

"What?" Sylvia asked, lifting her eyebrows and looking at me quizzically. "You just found yourself in a tough spot; you corrected your partner, and then you let that guy know you needed him to control his own dog. Seems to me that's exactly what you ought to do."

"Oh, I guess so!" I answered, muzzling the perfectionist in my head.

We settled on a bench, then, and watched the people and dogs around us. Orange, plastic cones marked off separate obedience rings. In the nearest one, a graceful border collie seemed to glide at its handler's side while a golden retriever pranced as if it were leading a marching band. A black Labrador performed with stellar precision, earning the highest marks in the ring.

I was fascinated by all of those canine

competitors; yet as I looked down at my own dog, now lying tranquilly at my feet, I knew I wouldn't trade him for all the obedience champions in the state.

To make our partnership official, Slugger and I had to complete one final task—'off-lead heeling.'

Sylvia directed us to take a walk up to the vendors' area. "Just work like you normally would and then let go of your leash. You want the dog to see that you're no longer holding it, but he should remain in heel position at all times."

"Got it!" I told Slugger to heel, and we made our way toward the brightly striped awnings where merchants were selling everything from canine clothing to pooper scoopers.

Then I dropped his leash; its leather end skipped across the dry grass as we walked. Slugger looked up at me. His eyebrows twitched. But he remained at my side, heeling perfectly. Suddenly a lump rose in my throat. My thoughts turned to the day several months ago—that incredible morning Slugger and I met and took our first awkward walk together.

I'd been so amazed when he heeled on leash. And now here he was, beside me, working, helping, and heeling, *without* that leash. I realized our partnership was changing; initially connected by lead and collar, it was now held together by something much more powerful—our deep and growing bond.

"Well done!" Sylvia called from behind me. Her words pulled me from my reverie. "I've seen enough to know y'all got that down pat. You can pick up the leash now."

I glanced back and grinned. Then I whispered to

my canine partner, "I think *you* should get it." I stopped walking and commanded, "Slugger, leash." My dog promptly grasped the end of the leather strap and delivered it to my waiting hand. "Good dog!" I exclaimed. The two of us circled back toward Vickie and Sylvia.

They were laughing when we reached them. "What's so funny?" I asked. Vickie slapped her hand over her mouth. I turned to Sylvia. "Want to let me in on it?" My question just made her laugh harder. The women's giggles combined with my relief at finishing our test and I began to snicker in spite of myself. "Come on; it's not nice to keep secrets, especially on certification day. Out with it!"

"Well, we were just noticing something about you and Slugger" Sylvia drawled. You're so in synch that when you walk, your . . . err . . . your butts wiggle the same way! And by the way, you passed your certification with flying colors." She threw her arms around me.

Wrapped in Sylvia's congratulatory hug, I couldn't speak. Her joke made me smile; yet her words also soothed a long-standing and painful wound in my heart. All my life I'd been told that the way I walked was bad, wrong, in need of fixing. I'd always believed that.

Yet in the time I'd spent with Slugger, I'd learned that being in unison with him was a *good* thing—a very good thing. The voice inside my mind whispered a new possibility: *maybe the way we move, the way I move, isn't bad at all.*

"Hugs all around." Vickie tapped my shoulder,

turned me gently in her direction. She was crying now, and tears slid down my own face. We'd all worked so hard to make this day a success; and we'd done it— Slugger and I were officially a team. Slugger would be going home with me tonight, for good!

This moment marked the start of something wonderful and profound in my life. But for Vickie it meant letting go, saying good-bye to Slugger. Embracing the dog's trainer, I whispered, "I'll take good care of him, I promise."

"I know." Vickie sniffed then swallowed hard. You'll both take care of each other. That's how it works."

Vickie's words echoed in my mind hours later, as I welcomed Slugger home. The big Lab trotted through each room of the house, sniffing, exploring, and poking his inquisitive nose into every corner. I unpacked his toys and set his food bowls in the pantry. "Hope you like the new digs!"

Slugger grabbed his favorite squashed soccer ball and pranced up to me. I swatted playfully at the black and white leather that stuck out from his mouth like a half-blown piece of bubble gum. The dog snorted, then followed me into my bedroom and plopped down in the middle of the floor. Gnawing on his ball, he watched intently as I set up his bed and crate. I grinned. "This look okay to you?"

Thwack, thwack, thwack came his wagged affirmation.

Slugger and I spent the remainder of our first evening together, just hanging out. By the time we'd enjoyed dinner and a fun game of fetch, we both welcomed the chance to relax on the front porch. I settled into a big wooden rocker, and Slugger stretched out at my feet.

A breeze moved through the boughs of the trees surrounding us, adding a gentle rustle to the chorus of tree frogs. Every now and then Slugger sighed and the deep, contented sounds seemed to resonate with the gladness in my own heart.

I listened to those same sighs as I drifted off to sleep later that night. I'd pulled Slugger's bed next to mine, and now I reached down until my fingers touched the softness of the dog's coat. Smiling, I whispered what would become my nightly promise: "Rest well, my sweet dog. I love you and I'll see you in the morning."

Chapter 7

The Good, the Bad, and the Dust Puppies

The triumph and tears of our certification left no doubt that Slugger was destined to make a difference in my life; yet even that momentous event could not reveal how great that difference would be. Such understanding could only come from experience. It had to be *lived* moment by moment.

My first summer with Slugger unfolded in my family's cabin on North Mountain. There, in the shade of towering oak trees and the pines Pop Pop had planted years ago, I discovered the day-to-day joys and challenges of our partnership.

Slugger was now my constant companion. His was the first face I saw each morning, and throughout the day the steady padding of his paws joined the lopsided thud of my footsteps.

Just as I had imagined on the day Sylvia first told me about Slugger, my dog stayed by my side even in the bathroom. One afternoon I reached down from my seat on the toilet to where Slugger was curled at my feet. I ran my fingers over the flaxen velvet of his muzzle. "So much for privacy, huh buddy?" I said.

Tail wag.

All at once I realized that this situation was familiar. My childhood days in the hospital had never offered much privacy. I learned early on that it's hard to pee when you're perched atop an ice-cold bedpan. I'd always thought that ought to be obvious to the nurses who took care of me, but they never seemed to get it. They would shove the frigid container beneath my bare buttocks and say, "Okay, go on and take a wee now."

Then they would stand there, waiting, just waiting, for me to pee. I didn't like doing it when I wasn't alone, but I closed my eyes and imagined being somewhere else until warm liquid slipped between my thighs. I told myself things would be better once my doctors let me get up out of bed. Then I'd be able to use a regular toilet again.

The girls' toilet was just down the hall from my room. It was a pink place. The walls, even the floor tiles, were the color of Pepto-Bismol. When I was ten years old and allowed to make my first post-op visit there, I decided the girls' bathroom was the nicest place I'd ever seen. It had toilets, real toilets, and though there weren't doors in front of them, there were curtains. These were long, the color of oatmeal. They didn't match the obnoxious pink around them. Still, I liked these curtains because they seemed to offer at least a little privacy.

With my full leg casts, I needed help in the

bathroom. My nurse called another woman to lend a hand, and between the two of them they managed to maneuver me into an empty stall and settle me on the toilet. I wasn't sitting so much as leaning on the seat, but I didn't mind. I thanked my nurse and the woman for their help. I smiled, hoping they would recognize my cue that meant, "You should leave now and let me pee in peace."

The women looked pleased to have gotten me— clunky casts and all—where I was supposed to be. They smiled back. But they didn't get my cue. They just stood in the pink and crowded stall, looking at me. A moment later my nurse said, "Okay, go on and take a wee."

Now, after years of being observed by medical staff during even my most personal moments, I was being watched by my dog. He stared at me with perked ears and an expression that seemed simultaneously loving and comical. And I didn't mind one bit.

Such togetherness was a practical and necessary part of the new bond I shared with Slugger; and just as Slugger accompanied me, a wake of white fur accompanied *him*. Despite regular brushings, hairs from the big Labrador's coat found their way into everything. They seemed to thrive in the places I used to call "dust-bunny hideouts." Now, wispy "dust puppies" took over every corner of the house.

Fine hairs stuck to my clothing, too. They clung most stubbornly to dark shirts, and even poked through the woven bands of my socks.

I learned to do a quick check at mealtimes. Was that a dog hair on my spoon? Atop my sandwich? On the rim of my drinking glass? Though I plucked away all the renegade fluff I saw, it was easy to imagine a gradually ingested stash of Labrador fur growing in some remote place in my gut.

Slugger was also concerned with his gut, but unlike me, he was interested in what went *in* rather than what should be kept out. Although most human food—with cheese being the notable exception—was off limits, Slugger adored his crunchy, bone-shaped treats and his twice-daily bowls of dog kibble.

I discovered just how passionate my dog was about mealtimes on a bright July morning. It was 7:30, nearing his 7:45 breakfast, and I was sipping my first cup of coffee. I reached for the TV remote and switched on my favorite news show. Slugger was lying on the floor nearby. "Can't seem to get awake," I mumbled to him as I nudged a spoon lazily around my coffee mug. The Lab didn't share my problem. He was bright-eyed and alert; at the sound of my voice, his tail swished across the kitchen tile.

The TV caught my attention then. One of the sunny program hosts smiled from behind a kitchen counter. Beside her, a swarthy fellow in an apron was making artichoke and mushroom calzones.

I was drawn to this culinary creativity—the carefully stretched rounds of pizza dough, the thinly sliced vegetables, the fresh thyme, chopped garlic, and blended cheeses—all destined for the preheated pizza stone. The chef built a calzone for the camera, deftly filling then folding it. He crimped the edges neatly with his fingers.

Suddenly my own fingers felt cold and wet. They'd been resting in my lap, and now Slugger was bumping them with his big nose. He stood there, bumped my hands, snorted, bumped them again. "What's up, boy?" I asked. The Labrador took a step back. He tossed his head to the right. The gesture was exaggerated and impatient. "Huh?" I said.

Slugger repeated the motion several times until I turned my head to follow his gaze. "What? There's nothing strange over there. Just the dishwasher, some cabinets, your . . . " Ah ha! My dog's food dish, his *empty* food dish, was sitting on the floor. Slugger was swinging his head, pointing at the metal bowl to remind me that it—like his stomach—needed filling.

He followed me, still snorting, as I walked over to his bag of dog food, scooped out breakfast, and poured water into the bowl. "Slugger, wait," I commanded. Drool slipped from the corners of his mouth. He gazed at his meal with a shark-like expression. The moment I said, "Okay," he dove into it, chomping and slurping.

Slugger's latest antics affirmed that, even at its most basic level, our partnership depended on communication. My brilliant dog seemed to understand this. He was good at conveying his needs. But I wasn't always adept at reading them.

One rainy afternoon a few weeks later, I was

relaxing on the couch when Slugger pranced up to me. He had just finished gnawing on a rawhide bone—a "welcome to the neighborhood" gift from a friend. Unbeknownst to me, my dog had eaten a large piece of this thoughtful but inexpensive treat. Now he rested his head in my lap. I scratched behind his ear. "Hey, Buddy!" I said. Slugger's tail waved, but I noticed an odd expression on his face. My dog's lips were pulled back in a way I'd never seen before. He looked as if he were grinning.

I was naïve and loving. "What is it, Sluggie?"

He tilted his head. He vomited all over my legs. "Oh Lord!" I exclaimed, jumping up and hurrying him out the front door. The poor Lab staggered into the yard. Rain pelted him as he heaved up his ill-ingested bone.

I followed him to the edge of the porch and wiped the smelly mess off my legs with an old towel. Then I joined Slugger in the grass.

I hated seeing the helper and companion I now adored, sick. Stroking his wet fur and talking softly, I did my best to comfort him. When Slugger's stomach finally calmed, I dried him off, took him inside and sat with him until I was convinced the crisis was over.

Never again, I vowed, would I give him a cheap rawhide.

I doubt he missed those inexpensive treats after his bad experience. But I soon found out he had a distinctly doggie penchant for something else. I discovered this just as I was waking up one morning. It all began with a mischievous canine snort. That snort brought a drowsy smile to my lips. Little did I know it also heralded the start of a game that was destined to become a ritual in my relationship with Slugger.

I gazed at my Labrador alarm clock through half-closed eyes. Slugger rested his big head on the edge of my mattress and peered at me expectantly. Extracting one hand from the cozy cocoon of my bed sheets, I reached out to deliver a good morning pet. "Hey, Buddy!"

My fingers danced across the softness of Slugger's head and then his muzzle before massaging the triangle of his ear. Slugger leaned into my touch. He tilted his head further and further toward the pleasure, until I was certain I was about to witness the world's first canine headstand. Just then my big yellow dog let out a long, loud moan. I laughed. "Is that just the *best* feeling ever?"

I was so caught up in the moment of canine comedy that I didn't quite grasp what happened next. Slugger took a step back. He ducked his head out of sight. I was puzzled. "What are you after down there, boy?"

When he emerged from his bedside dive a moment later, I had my answer. Wispy bits of dust and fluff clung to his whiskers like tiny acrobats; tucked in his mouth was a sock. I had put it by my bed along with its mate the night before, and now it peeked out from between my Labrador's jaws.

Slugger apparently hoped to keep it a secret; he pulled his jowls quickly down over his ill-gotten booty and looked at me sweetly.

"Don't think I don't know what you've got!" I said, trying to sound serious. "You better give me that sock!"

Slugger's tail wagged furiously. He closed his mouth tightly around his stolen treasure and blinked at me. Then he began to back away from the bed. I watched in amazement as my usually devoted and hard-working service dog continued his backward shuffle toward the bedroom door.

Suddenly it hit me—I was witnessing a robbery in progress! "Get back here, sock-napper!"

Slugger ignored my words. With that stolen sock now dangling crazily from his mouth, he turned and bolted from the bedroom. I heard him race down the hallway. The thunderous noise conveyed his rump-in-the-air, whiskers-to-the-wind getaway.

Given my wobbly legs, hot pursuit was out of the question, so I chose the next best thing—a cool head. I slid out of bed and ventured toward the living room, fully expecting to find eighty-five pounds of canine tenacity guarding my sock.

Instead I found Slugger lying next to the couch, cradling a perfectly legal rubber bone between his paws. I sidled up to him and looked 'round the contours of his body to see if the loot might be pinned beneath an elbow or flattened against his belly. I scanned the living room, the hallway. Nothing.

Slugger looked up at me with a wide-eyed, adoring

gaze that seemed to say, *Sock? What sock? Not seen any of those 'round here.* He thumped his tail.

I wasn't buying it. "Okay, Mr. Sock Breath, where'd you put it?" I demanded.

He perked his ears in my direction. He stretched. He stood up. For a moment I thought he was going to retrieve my pilfered garment. Maybe . . . but then Slugger lay down on the braided rug and let out a huge yawn.

I imagined myself like a special investigator interrogating a suspect. "Well you know you'd be better off cooperating with me here, buddy." I paused for effect. "Why not make it easy on yourself? All you have to do is bring me the sock. Just bring it back, and all will be fine."

Slugger snorted. He turned his attention to his bone and began gnawing it vigorously. The message was clear; the canine thief wasn't about to crack under pressure.

Very well, I thought. *If Slugger can feign indifference to all this, then so can I.* I switched my thoughts to breakfast and polished off a bowl of cereal and a glass of orange juice before stacking my dishes in the sink.

Slugger watched me as I sauntered into the study at the other end of the house. I settled at my desk, reached beneath it, and flipped the power switch of my computer.

My gaze tracked these familiar movements. But then something unusual caught my eye. "What the heck?" I muttered. Squinting, I leaned down and looked into the furthest corner under the desk.

The whoop that passed through my lips when I

recognized my crumpled, slobber-logged sock brought Slugger galloping into the study. He lifted his eyebrows inquiringly. I couldn't help myself; like the winner in a child's game of hide-and-seek, I sang out, "I found the sock! I found the sock!" I waggled my finger playfully in the dog's face. "Hah, I win! That means you have to creep under there and get the prize for me. Go on now; get it."

The pilferer-with-paws was gracious in defeat. He retrieved the sock with poise—or at least with as much poise as he could muster while crawling on his belly with a sock sticking out of his mouth. He placed his treasure obediently in my lap. Then he nuzzled my hand, woofed, and wagged his entire back end.

"Thank you, rascal!" I chortled. As I ruffled Slugger's ears, I wondered what had inspired this impromptu game. I didn't find the answer that morning, or the next, or any morning after that.

Perhaps sock-nappings were simply Slugger's way of ensuring each day got off to a fun start. Yet our quirky morning ritual held valuable lessons as well. In the summer of my twenty-third year I learned not to take my socks for granted. And not to take myself too seriously.

One morning, not long after a sock-napping session, I found myself facing another lesson—and I learned this one the hard way. Slugger had just finished his breakfast and was staring at me, bouncing up and down on his front paws. By now I recognized the signal—it was my dog's way of letting me know he'd like a potty break. "You need to go outside?" I asked and he hopped faster. Affirmative.

The moment I let him out, he scampered over to his favorite bush and peed on it. I watched from the door as he ambled across the yard, looking around, sniffing, and taking his time. *Well* I thought, *if Slugger needs to take a dump, he's in no hurry.* I decided to let him stay outside a bit longer so that he could take care of business in his own good time, but I wasn't in the mood to stay there and keep an eye on him.

You really should get the kitchen straightened, Leigh, the perfectionist in my head said. My cereal bowl still sat on the counter; a few soggy Cheerios floated forlornly in the leftover milk I'd been too picky to finish off. Orange pips clung to the rim of my empty juice glass, and there were so many toast crumbs on the table that it looked as if Hansel and Gretel had stopped by for a morning visit.

"Back in a minute," I called to Slugger. He was still nosing around the far end of the yard, and he glanced back at the sound of my voice. My bare feet slapped against the tile floor as I hurried into the kitchen. Collecting my dirty dishes, I filled the sink with warm, soapy water and dumped them in. I wiped off the table and counters then washed and dried the dishes and put them away. The chores were simple and I thought I'd made quick work of them, but when I went to the front door to let my dog back in the house, I didn't see him.

I peered around the yard, beyond the far side of the porch, up and down the driveway. Slugger wasn't there. "Crap!" Tender-footed and annoyed, I walked to the edge of the porch and called, "Sluggie, come! Time to come inside now, boy! Sluggie! Sluggie!" I expected to hear the jangle of his collar as he returned to me at an obedient gallop, but when my voice quieted, only the summer insects answered.

This was odd; he normally stayed well within the yard, and he'd always been quick to come when I hailed him. I dashed back into the house and slipped my feet into the first pair of tennis shoes I could find. Tying them quickly, I went out the back door, calling him more loudly, more urgently than before. I trekked slowly all the way around the yard. My eyes searched for a spot of Labrador yellow amid the greens of grass and trees. Still nothing.

Now panic began to bubble up in my brain. *What's happened? Where the hell can he be?* I went around to the front porch and plopped into a rocking chair. I thought perhaps I should sit there for a bit, catch my breath, and wait for Slugger to show up. That sounded like a reasonable approach, but I was too anxious to be still. I grabbed the car keys and headed out.

Driving slowly up and down the mountain road that wound past the cabin, I stuck my head out the window. I yelled for Slugger. The voice in my head screeched all the while, *What were you thinking? You should have kept an eye on him, idiot!* I had messed up. And now the dog that had been as close as my shadow for all these weeks was missing. "Damn it!" I hissed.

Perhaps Slugger's keen ears had picked up my frantic calls or the familiar rumble of the car's engine. Or maybe while I was out scouring the countryside for him, he simply decided it was time to head home. I couldn't say what had motivated his return, but when I finally pulled the car into the driveway, he was standing there, wagging and panting. Tears spilled down my cheeks when I noticed a goofy canine grin on his brown face.

Wait a minute! Slugger was a *yellow* Lab. With a brown face? "What in tarnation?" I cried. Leaping from the car, I stumbled toward him, only to realize that more than his head was brown—a good three quarters of his body was now umber. I was nearly inspired to deliver a witty one-liner about impersonating a chocolate Lab, but a foul stench quelled the humor. My beloved canine reeked as if he had just crawled out of a sewer.

I slapped a hand to my forehead, suddenly seeing the big picture. My sneaky pal must have cut through the woods on the edge of the property and made his way down to the neighbor's farm. That farm had an expansive pasture with a pond for a sizeable herd of cattle. The wet, stinking muck all over Slugger's coat left little to the imagination; he'd clearly enjoyed a good old-fashioned romp, helping himself to all the cow shit, mud, and scummy pond water he could manage.

Holding my breath to avoid the smell, I crept closer. Slugger trotted jauntily up to me. He leaned against my legs and tilted his head back. His eyes twinkled, his tongue lolled out one side of his mouth. He was the canine embodiment of joyful abandon.

With disgusting sludge now coating my legs, I couldn't share his mischievous enthusiasm. Remnants of the fear and anger I'd felt that morning suddenly swelled within me. They merged with my relief, creating a bizarre kaleidoscope of emotion. Half of me wanted to strangle Slugger; half of me wanted to hug him and never let go.

Fortunately, common sense prevailed, and I chose neither option. Instead I went around to the side of the cabin to fetch the garden hose. "Come on, you little turd," I fussed at Slugger, "I'm not letting you out of my sight!"

By the time I'd rinsed the top layer of crud from his fur, lathered him with copious amounts of shampoo, and scrubbed every inch of him three times, his top-of-the-world demeanor had disappeared. Although he did not turn belligerent or try to escape, Slugger kept his ears flat and his head down while I worked.

He clearly thought the sooner this process was over, the better. "Sorry, bud," I said, rinsing him for the fourth and final time. "This is the price you pay for running off and frolicking in the crap!"

With his forlorn expression and his drippy fur slicked against his body, he suddenly looked more like a drowned rat than a respectable service animal. But a good toweling off perked up his coat as well as his mood.

For as much as he despised being washed, Slugger *loved* being dried. He snorted and groaned with pleasure as I worked the towel over his legs and belly. When I dried his back, he wagged so fiercely I wondered how he managed to stay upright.

My own back needed a break. Having bent over Slugger for what felt like eons, I stood up slowly and carefully. "Just need to uncrick my spine," I told him, shaking out his towel and sending water droplets and fur flying through the air. As if inspired by the flapping towel, he suddenly charged off the porch. He careened around the yard with his tail tucked and his butt in the air. After three full-throttle laps, he charged at the towel like the bull in a bullfight.

"Hah!" I guffawed. "You want to play bullfight after all this? I love you, but don't push your luck!"

As summer stretched toward autumn, the canine recipient of my love took his own devotion in an unexpected direction. It happened early one August morning. I was relaxing in the hammock that hung on the front porch, keeping an eye on Slugger while he enjoyed our surroundings in a more paws-on fashion.

He'd begun this day as he had most others that summer, making his way along the perimeter of the yard. With his powerful nose scouring the ground, he'd resembled a Labrador detective, carefully inspecting every inch of the boundary between the lawn and the forest.

But this morning my yellow dog returned from

his customary walk later than usual. "What kept you out there so long today, Sluggie?" I asked as he trotted up to the porch. I reached out to give him a pat. That's when I realized he was carrying something. I thought perhaps he'd discovered some extraordinary fetching stick or maybe some long-forgotten tennis ball. I was wrong. Clutched between Slugger's powerful jaws was a turtle!

The creature huddled safe within its dirty shell. No doubt it hoped its career as a dog toy would be a short one. As for Slugger, he was clearly convinced that his latest discovery was a rare treasure, indeed. His eyes sparkled, and great joyful wags danced across his entire body. I couldn't help laughing at my dog's exhilaration. Still, I wondered what he would do next.

After turning in circles three times, Slugger lay down on the porch next to me. He held the muddy turtle between his front paws. I was prepared to intervene if he started to gnaw on its hard outer covering. But I need not have worried. My fastidious dog grasped the turtle carefully and started *licking* its mud-caked shell.

Squishy slurping sounds filled the air as Slugger licked and licked. He did not stop until that shell glistened. When the apparent housecleaning was complete, my dog stretched out for a nap beside his turtle. He did not leave his post until I called him into the house.

Once left to its own devices, Slugger's shell-bearing buddy trudged off the porch. By evening, it was nowhere in sight. I did not expect to see that turtle anymore, but I was wrong. Again.

The very next day, Slugger returned from his usual morning jaunt carrying the same little turtle in his mouth. Just as before, he settled on the porch with the turtle between his paws, and the timid creature stayed hidden in its shell while Slugger gave it another thorough spit shine.

Amazingly, this routine continued for nearly two weeks until Slugger and I headed to graduate school.

When we left the peaceful cabin and the respite of the Blue Ridge Mountains, we also said good-bye to one little turtle who probably smelled like dog slobber for weeks after we were gone. Yet my first, eye-opening summer with Slugger brought me lasting lessons about real life and real love. More would soon follow.

Chapter 8

Big Dog on Campus

Graduate school found Slugger filling yet another role in my life. The versatile dog who was my assistant, my buddy, and my personal comedian, became my college roommate. The moment the two of us set foot and paw inside the residence hall that would serve as our home-away-from-home, we were surrounded by our new neighbors.

While I said hello to my hall-mates, Slugger got busy charming every dog-loving girl in the building. He answered each sweetly-crooned greeting with a captivating glance and his most winsome wag. By the time I had my belongings unpacked, it seemed my Labrador already had his own fan club.

At the opening hall meeting later that night, the would-be members of his fast-growing club cooed at Slugger and periodically broke into impromptu exclamations. "Oh, what a doll! Have you ever seen such beautiful eyes? And look how *good* he's being!" I couldn't blame my hall-mates for their fascination with Slugger, any more than I could help feeling pleased and proud to witness it.

When it was my turn to officially introduce myself to the room full of curious faces, confidence buoyed my words.

"My name is Leigh, and I happen to have the world's greatest roommate. This is my service dog, Slugger." He was seated beside me. I reached over and patted his head before uttering the truth I'd kept silent for most of my life. "I have a disability called cerebral palsy. Slugger's been specially trained to assist with tasks I have trouble doing on my own. He helps me keep my balance when I walk, and he carries my belongings. He'll also turn lights on and off for me and retrieve stuff I drop. If I need him to, Slugger will even take things back and forth between me and another person."

I would have launched into a lengthier speech about Slugger's skills had it not been for the ripple of amazement that suddenly spread through the gathering.

"So you mean you can tell the dog to come take something from me and bring it to *you*? You're foolin', right?" A girl in plaid boxers and a T-shirt tossed her questions at me and grinned as if I'd just told her the punch line of a really good joke.

I grinned back at her. "Nope, I'm not kidding."

"How 'bout this, then?" She waved a purple JMU keychain in the air.

"Sure. If you hold it down at Slugger's level, I'll have him retrieve it." When she'd placed the object on her palm and extended it in front of her, I alerted him.

Pointing directly at the keychain, I said, "Slugger, take it!"

He seemed eager to demonstrate his skills. He trotted over, scooped the keychain carefully into his mouth, and returned to me. At my command, he dropped it in my lap.

"Good boy!" I praised him and fed him a piece of cheese before telling him to lie down once more. I wiped the keychain on the corner of my shirt to remove the slobber. Then I held it up. "See?" But now my voice was barely audible; it was drowned out by thunderous applause.

Slugger's eager assistance at the hall meeting brought him acclaim; more importantly, it earned him the respect of my hall-mates. Friends often visited my sociable Lab when he was off duty.

They sought him out for help with everything from study breaks to break-ups. Nonetheless, my neighbors understood that Slugger was much more than a cuddly companion. They learned to practice restraint when he was dressed and working.

Even his most ardent admirers stilled their friendly fingers as they read the "Please Do Not Pet" signs on his harness.

My own bond with Slugger flourished in our day-to-day life at JMU. That bond re-shaped ordinary moments. With him beside me, getting from place to place was easier than I had ever hoped it could be. "Mind going with me to pick up dinner?" I asked him one evening as I clicked the lead onto his collar.

Slugger's tail assumed its steady working wag. Together we left our dorm and trekked across campus.

Our route held countless obstacles for my wobbly legs; when I found myself at the top of a steep concrete staircase, my palms began to sweat. The steps that snaked their way to Mr. Jazzy's, my favorite campus eatery, reminded me of all the excruciating tumbles I'd taken on stairs just like these.

As a child I'd loved nothing better than to retreat to the basement of our house. I stacked pillows and stuffed animals on the cool floor there and imagined being the heroine in a constantly unfolding drama I called *Little House on the Cushion*.

I wore my mother's old nightgowns. I loved the way they felt, how they flounced and shimmered as I moved. I slipped my bare feet into shiny high-heels that were way too big for me, so I shoved my toes as far forward as they would go.

Clomping around the basement, I practiced refined smiles and held long conversations with the imaginary playmates I called Jiffy and Piggy.

From upstairs, my mother would dutifully remind me when it was time for me to take off my shoes. My doctors had told her that high heels would worsen the problems in my feet and legs, so I was only allowed to borrow their elegance for a few minutes each day. "Oh, Jiffy, oh Piggy!" I'd proclaim to my make-believe friends, "I don't want to take the lovely high heels off. I want to keep them on forever!"

One day, in a flash of inspiration, I shuffled toward the wooden staircase. I'd been warned not to climb those stairs by myself, but I was determined. Maybe if I managed to stroll upstairs in my dress-up shoes, my mother would realize that they were not bad for me at all. I crouched low to keep my balance and began creeping up each step, the heels of my shiny shoes flopping behind me. The smooth soles slid as if I were moving across ice. Still, I had to do this. I inched forward, willing myself up one step and then the next.

At last I saw the tired white linoleum of our kitchen floor stretched out in front of me. I'd almost made it. I had to seem as if I'd blithely skipped upstairs to find out what we'd be having for lunch, so I groped the walls and fought to stand up straight. Pulling myself upright, I instinctively stepped back to find my balance, but there was no balance to find.

I pitched backward and bit my tongue as my body crashed down the steps. I glimpsed the weird tangle of my arms and legs, heard the repeated thumping of my skull against the steps, at last felt the coolness of the basement floor against my face. Then there was nothing but black.

The memory of such terrifying falls made my heart race. But now, as if sensing my dread, Slugger moved in close to give me extra stability on the steps. I smiled. "What a good boy you are!" My praise quickened the tempo of Slugger's waving tail—a few joyous allegro *thwacks* cut in on the sedate rhythm of his working wag.

He looked up at me. His brown eyes sparkled with a sure and simple message. "Take hold."

Letting go of my fear, I gripped the raised leather handle of his harness and proceeded down the first step. Slugger stood motionless, supporting me, until I was safely on the stair below him. Only after I'd said, "Okay" did he follow me down. The two of us took each step this way, moving slowly and precisely.

The smell of frying hamburgers hung in the air as a red-haired girl hurried through the exit of Mr. Jazzy's. She looked up at us and grinned. "Way cool!"

Stepping onto the sidewalk, I nodded. "Thanks. It's all about teamwork!"

That teamwork steadied my wobbly movements each time Slugger and I traveled to and from the scattered buildings of our academic world. Once inside those buildings, his paws tapped a reassuring rhythm through tiled corridors.

The slick and shiny floors had once been perilous for me, but when I held his harness, I felt secure and independent. The dog that made those feelings possible also inspired an outward change. Moving through bustling hallways and crowded classrooms, I held my head up. And I smiled.

"You sure look happy!" My friend Sean remarked as the two of us slid into adjacent desks and prepared for our 7 p.m. Family Systems class.

"Yeah," I teased. "What can I say? Night classes always fill me with joy."

"I know what you mean." Sean returned the joke, "Think of all those unfortunate saps who have to stay home tonight and do nothing but chill out on the sofa and watch TV." Then he glanced down at Slugger, who was resting beside my desk with his head propped on my foot. "Well at least *some* of us can relax, huh, boy?" Slugger lifted one eyebrow. He flipped his tail in a solitary wag of acknowledgement.

"His head is so heavy, I think my foot's going to fall asleep!" I proclaimed.

Just then, our course instructor scuttled into the room. A haphazard tower of papers and books teetered in her arms. Sean leaned toward me and whispered, "You'll be lucky if your foot is the *only* thing that falls asleep. It looks like we're in for a long evening!" As I opened my binder and began taking notes, I had a feeling my friend was right.

When we took a break an hour and a half later, I felt as if my eyelids had turned to lead. Struggling to keep them raised, I sought out the nearest vending machine. I deposited a handful of coins, pressed a brightly-lit button, and a Mountain Dew clunked to the slot near my feet. Ah, caffeine! I laced my fingers around the cold metal can, grateful for the sweet, fizzy contents that would get me through the remainder of my night class.

While I swigged soda and got back to the business of taking notes, Slugger curled up on the floor beside my desk. I knew it wouldn't be long before he was courting the Sandman. I couldn't blame him; the night seemed to stretch out interminably as the hands on the generic wall clock dragged from one minute to the next.

By the final half hour of class, exhaustion hung in the air as thick as London fog. My bleary-eyed classmates and I did our best to stay focused, but for Slugger, it was just too much. Lulled by our professor's hushed monotone, he fell asleep—completely and deeply asleep. Slugger's lip lifted ever so slightly as he slid into a dream. His paws twitched.

Then, a sound, a sonorous rumble, welled up. It rose above the professor's voice, above the studious scratching of pens and pencils.

Suddenly it seemed as if someone had pressed a pause button, freezing everything in the room. Writing instruments stilled. The professor stopped speaking. Then she glared at me with eyes that looked ready to launch arrows.

"Sorry, guess I better wake my dog," I said, reaching down and nudging Slugger.

"Oh!" The instructor's angry expression gave way to a look of sheepish confusion. She stood silently for what seemed like an eternity, before finally sighing and offering a tired half-smile. "I guess I can take the hint." Glancing around at her drowsy students, she added, "Technically we should keep working for twenty more minutes, but you heard the dog. Let's call it a night."

Minutes later we filed down the hall and through the building's heavy glass doors. "Sure is great having Slugger in class!" Sean said. Like most of my friends and classmates, he regarded Slugger with both appreciation and respect.

But it wasn't long before I was reminded that not everyone would hold Slugger or our partnership in such high esteem.

Slugger and I were in the campus post office

when a stranger asked, "Hey dog, you want a bite?" He began waving a greasy potato chip just beyond Slugger's whiskers.

Instinctively, I put my hand in front of Slugger's mouth to block the temptation. "Please don't bother him. He's working."

A flashy, jeweled *M* hung around the neck of the potato-chip bearer. It swayed on its heavy gold chain when he laughed. "Yeah, looks like he's working real hard." Sarcasm dripped from his words. "M" nudged a lanky guy standing next to him. "Isn't that dog just standin' there?"

"Yeah, sure." M's buddy seemed unconvinced and uncomfortable. He shifted his weight from one leg to the other then shoved the toe of his trendy athletic shoe against the tiled floor so that it squeaked sharply. "Come on, man, I'm thirsty," he said, loping off in the direction of the nearest vending machine.

M tossed the last of his chips into his mouth. "Whatever." He looked down at Slugger. "Working, my ass," he muttered. With that, he jogged off to join his friend.

I was waiting for a postal clerk to bring me some stamps when my ears detected a now familiar voice. "Still say the dog's working?" M leaned languidly against a nearby chair. I glared at him and he sneered, "Bet I can change that." He plunged his hand into the depths of his orange duffel bag and pulled out a tennis ball. Then he let it slip from his fingers.

Slugger's ears perked; his head bobbed gently, following the path of the ball as it *plonked* repeatedly against the floor. M laughed. Finally he grabbed the fluorescent yellow orb. "Is this what you want? You like this, boy? Huh?" he taunted, waving the tennis ball slowly through the air.

"Slugger, leave it," I said. "Down." Slugger glanced up at me, smacked his lips once, and obeyed. I turned on M and looked him straight in the eye. In a calm and stern voice I ordered, "Quit bothering my dog, jerk!"

"Geez, okay then!" M shot back. With a single swift motion, he knelt down and rolled the tennis ball in Slugger's direction. Slugger's eyes widened as it spun toward him and grazed his front paw, but he didn't move. At last the felt-covered sphere came to an abrupt halt against the side of a postal clerk's shoe.

The clerk, a tall, smiling man who often assisted me, had come around from the back of the post office to bring me the stamps I needed. "Here you go," he said. Then he picked up the tennis ball. Dusting it with his palm, he handed it to me. "I reckon your hard-working partner has earned this!"

"Oh yes!" I stuffed the ball into Slugger's backpack and grinned triumphantly at M. His smirk was gone. A moment later, so was he. I was still smiling as I headed back to my dorm with one book of stamps, one dedicated service dog, and one *very* well-deserved tennis ball.

Watching Slugger gnaw on his newest treasure later that evening, I realized that this special friend who helped me walk was simultaneously helping me stand up. Slowly and steadily I *was* learning to stand up—for him, for our partnership, and even for myself.

Chapter 9

When Pigs Fly

"Would your dog like a pretzel?"

Slugger and I were walking home from class one afternoon when the question stopped us in our tracks. A guy I'd never seen before was crunching a snack stick and smiling at me. I thanked him for his generosity before explaining that human food was off-limits for my working partner.

"Okay, would *you* like a pretzel then?" he asked. I wasn't hungry, but this handsome stranger intrigued me, so I took him up on his offer. The two of us chatted, and by the time I'd enjoyed a handful of pretzels, I'd discovered that my new friend's name was Pranav. He was an international graduate student from India and was finishing his masters in Computer Science.

In the days following our first brief meeting, I kept an eye open for Pranav whenever I went out. To my delight, I discovered he was doing a graduate assistantship in the psychology department.

He was responsible for making sure all the computers there ran smoothly; I often found him tinkering with machines in the computer lab or scurrying between the psych professors' offices.

He'd grin when he saw me and Slugger. "Hi Leigh, hi Slugger!" Pranav's soft accent and the enthusiasm in his voice when he greeted us made my heart skip a beat.

Although the two of us clearly came from very different backgrounds, we soon realized we'd had some similar experiences. One afternoon, as we sat talking, Pranav gazed down at Slugger. "Such an incredible dog," he said. He paused for a moment before reflecting, "My grandfather would have loved him."

I listened wide-eyed as my friend told me about his *Papi*—a shrewd businessman who built his own soda company in India, and whose dearth of common sense was usually offset by his devotion to those he loved.

Not least among Papi's beloved were two huge Alsatians named Patsy and Rovey. A smile crossed my lips when Pranav said, "As a kid I learned to respect and love creatures by watching my grandfather with his animals." Thinking of my own grandfather, Pop Pop, I nodded.

So it seemed only fitting that Slugger should end up playing a prominent role in our first "official" date, a few days later. Instead of planning to go to a movie or a cozy coffee shop, Pranav and I agreed to meet outside on the quad after my night class. I promised to bring along a tennis ball and take Slugger out of his harness, so that we could all enjoy a good, old-fashioned game of fetch!

Pranav said he was looking forward to spending time with me and with Slugger in regular dog mode. Still, as I primped in front of a mirror before my class on our chosen evening, butterflies swooped and dived in my stomach. That was a familiar sensation, especially when it came to dating. I'd been nervous around guys for nearly as long as I'd been attracted to them.

One evening when I was in high school, I'd tried to calm my nerves by focusing on the tranquil light cast by the bedside lamp in my parents' room; but the phone that sat on the nearby nightstand stole my attention. Quietly I coached myself, *If you want to ask Wade to the Sadie Hawkins dance, you're going to have to call him.*

The thought of Sadie Hawkins made me smile. The Lil' Abner character got a dance named after her all because her pappy arranged a foot race so that she and other single gals could pursue the bachelors of Dogpatch. Those they caught, they married. *Imagine getting a fellow in a foot race!* I thought. *If that were how things worked these days, I'd be shit out of luck. Boy, I'm glad we use telephones!*

Inspired by this realization, I lifted the beige receiver from its cradle. I punched my pointer finger into the numbered circles of the rotary dial and thought about Wade. Though he wasn't exactly handsome in the hunky sort of way, I'd been drawn to his boyish good looks. They seemed to fit his friendly personality.

I was glad Wade and I were in many of the same classes since that meant I got to spend lots of time around him. His speedy correct answers in third period Calculus, coupled with his comic remarks when we reviewed *Macbeth* in English Literature, convinced me he was both smart and funny. My kind of guy!

Would Wade think I was his kind of girl? I held my breath as the phone rang on the other end of the line.

"Hello?" A woman answered. I assumed this was his mom and tried to adopt a relaxed yet respectful tone. "Yes, hi. Could I speak to Wade, please?"

"Sure, just a minute. I'll get him." There was a clunk as she put the phone down, then muffled voices. I wondered what they were saying. Tracing my fingers nervously around the dense plastic curls of the phone cord, I waited.

"Hey, Wade here."

Suddenly I felt like a kid on a roller coaster— gripped by the panic that hits just as the ride crests its first big hill. "Hey Wade, it's Leigh. How are you?" The voice inside my head kept chanting, *Try to sound cool. Try to sound cool.*

"I'm good." Wade answered. "What's up?"

I flirted momentarily with the idea of chickening out. I could say I was calling just to say hi or that I had a question about calculus homework. But then, driven by a heady mix of lust and courage, I forged ahead. "You know the Sadie Hawkins Dance is coming up. I was wondering if you'd like to go together."

There was a pause—a long pause—and I felt the blood rushing to my face. *At least*, I thought, *Wade can't see me blush.*

Finally, he spoke. "Well, actually, Teresa already asked me." He cleared his throat, then added, "But thanks for thinking of me."

I feigned complete indifference and wanted to make a quick exit. "Um, sure, just an idea. Well, I reckon I should let you get back to your evening."

"Yeah, guess so. See you tomorrow. And like I said, thanks."

"Sure." I hung up.

Switching off the lamp, I flopped onto my parents' bed. I was grateful to be alone. To counter my disappointment and embarrassment, I whispered a quick and numbing lie. "It doesn't matter." But as I lay in the darkness, the fresh memory of my conversation with Wade slowly gave way. It merged with a harsh and familiar message—one I'd heard over and over since I donned my first training bra. For years these words played in my head like a bad recording with the volume pushed all the way up. *"No guy wants a cripple."*

Now I drew an eye shadow wand across a small tile of dusty blue powder and leaned into the mirror where my breath made warm clouds on its surface. Though I'd never been much for the traditional dating scene, this evening I was determined not to listen to the unhealthy message of my earlier years. "That's bullshit!" I proclaimed, banishing it from my thoughts as I touched the tip of the wand to my eyelid.

Slugger was standing in the doorway behind me. I turned, bent down to him, and batted my eyes dramatically. "What do you think of this shade?"

His tail beat an enthusiastic confirmation against the door. "It's unanimous then!" I declared. As I sat through my long and tedious class later that evening, I blinked my pale blue eyelids and thought of little besides the friend I would see when class finally ended.

There was only one problem with my plan. Though I'd promised to furnish a tennis ball for the evening's entertainment, I'd been unable to find one in my room. I'd had no choice but to substitute Slugger's favorite stuffed toy.

When I met Pranav and pulled that squishy fuchsia pig from Slugger's backpack, I feared our date might come to an untimely end. Pranav scrunched his face into a scowl that left little doubt he was thinking, *Eeew gross!* But all he said was, "Um, what's that?"

"It's a pig! See?" I held the crumpled toy toward him, snout first. "Couldn't seem to locate a tennis ball before class, so I figured Sluggie could just fetch this."

Pranav nodded hesitantly but Slugger responded

without reservation; his eyes seemed to bore through the pig with an intense and feral stare.

"Hang on, wild beast!" I unfastened Slugger's harness and slipped it over his head. "In the mood for some fetch, huh?" My Labrador gave a mighty shake, and white fur danced in the air around him like blowing snow.

"So this is what he's like when he's not working," Pranav said. He reached down to pet Slugger, who was now spinning in crazy, excited circles. Obviously thrilled to be off duty and with a new friend, Slugger promptly snorted in my date's hand.

"Yep, he's all dog," I said. "Need a Kleenex?"

"That's okay." Pranav wiped his slimed fingers on his jeans, and as if to corroborate my statement, Slugger took the opportunity to sniff his crotch.

"He doesn't waste any time when it comes to introductions, either," I said with a quick laugh.

Pranav gave me a good-natured grin. "I noticed." He thumped Slugger's sides playfully.

"Time to get some wiggles out!" I waved the stuffed pig in the air and my dog jumped up on his hind legs. Every fiber of his being wanted that toy. The instant I tossed it, he streaked across the grass.

"Wow," Pranav exclaimed. "I'm used to seeing your dog walking calmly with you, but he can really get the lead out!"

I nodded. When Slugger pranced up, I grabbed a corner of his soggy toy and yanked it. "Give me that!" I squeaked. He lowered the front half of his body in a play bow. He kept a tight hold on his end of the pig and growled as we tugged back and forth. Finally, with my arms exhausted, I stopped pulling. Holding my hands still, I used my normal voice and said, "Slugger, give." The big Lab had a frenzied look in his eyes. Clearly he wasn't ready to end our tug of war; he kept his jaws clamped around his toy. "Give," I repeated more firmly.

Now Slugger relinquished his toy and backed up, waiting for the next throw. I tried to hurl it a long way, but this time my fingers wouldn't let go when I meant for them to, and the pig only hovered in the air a moment before landing on the ground just a few feet away. "Sometimes I can't throw worth a damn," I told Pranav.

"Well your dog doesn't seem to mind," he answered, moving closer to me. "The way you two interact, it's just amazing."

"Thanks! Want to throw a few?" I took the bedraggled toy from Slugger, passed it to Pranav.

"Sure." He pitched it far across the lawn.

I gasped. "Whoa, now that's what I call a powerful throw!"

Pranav grinned. "I threw the javelin in high school."

No wonder the pig was flying! Slugger raced joyfully after it. He snatched his toy out of the air without breaking stride. Panting and wagging, he returned and dropped it at Pranav's feet. His bright-eyed expression seemed to be the canine equivalent of "Do that again!"

So we did. Pranav and I took turns throwing the slobber-covered stuffed pig. We laughed and talked as we watched Slugger dash back and forth across the empty quad. By the time the towering street lamps spilled their light across the grass, my retriever was exhausted. I snapped the leash onto his collar and patted his head. "Well that was quite a fetch session!"

Pranav glanced down at my hands. "Are you cold? Your fingers look a bit blue."

In truth I'd been cold for the last hour, but I was so enamored with my new friend that I'd ignored the sensation. "Yeah, I am kind of chilly," I said now.

Smiling, Pranav took my right hand in both of his. "Any better?"

"Yes, thanks."

I wondered if he knew that his gentle gesture warmed my heart as well as my fingers—he kept his hand clasped around mine as we walked back to my dorm. With Slugger on one side of me and Pranav on the other, I felt content and giddy at the same time. It was a curious sensation to be sure. And I liked it.

When we reached the main doors of my building I offered, "All I have is a little room of my own, but you're welcome to come in and wash your hands if you want."

"That'd be great; they are pretty slobbery." Pranav followed me down the hall, and I ushered him into my cozy room. It was in need of tidying, but I directed him toward the bathroom, hoping he wouldn't pay attention to the mess. For Slugger, a guest meant the chance to show off the things he loved. While Pranav washed his hands, the Lab put on a parade featuring a stuffed frog, one of my black dress shoes, and two of the elusive tennis balls I'd been unable to locate earlier.

"Hambone dog!" Laughing, I scooped up his treasures and put them away. Then I closed and latched the door to my closet. He had a habit of nosing his way into the basket that held my dirty laundry there. He often pulled out my underwear, and I didn't want Pranav to encounter Slugger's version of a Victoria's Secret display on our first date.

"Make yourself comfortable," I said, when he returned from the bathroom. Pranav smiled and sat on my daybed as I hurried to the sink and de-slobbered my hands. Grabbing a bag of goldfish crackers from atop my tiny fridge, I sat down beside Pranav and offered them to him. "Need a snack?"

But all at once there was more between Pranav and me than goldfish. Slugger hopped onto the bed and promptly settled himself right in the middle of us. He was normally allowed on the furniture by invitation only, but had apparently appointed himself our canine chaperone. I could imagine him supervising like an underpaid teacher at a school dance: "Okay now everyone listen up; remember to keep at least a dog's width between you at all times!"

Funny as that vision was, I understood his actions. He'd not been trained to defend me, yet he took our partnership, and his part in it, very seriously. I often let my doctors, dentists, hairdressers—anyone who had close physical contact with me—say hello to Slugger on our first visit.

I was pleased when these folks viewed that allowance as a treat. Still, my primary concern was for my dog; I wanted him to realize he didn't have to worry when professionals tended to me.

Now I felt it was important to offer him a similar reassurance. Slugger had gotten accustomed to seeing Pranav while he worked. Our evening of fetch had also been positive and fun, and I figured that letting Slugger simply hang out with us as we chatted would boost his comfort level even further. I petted him as Pranav and I sat talking and munching cheese crackers.

Suddenly Pranav popped one of those crackers into Slugger's mouth. The dog gulped it down. Then he sat straight up, staring at his benefactor with the hard, shark-like look normally reserved for his dinner bowl. He wanted more! Long strings of drool dripped from his jowls.

Afraid that my cheese-loving hound might decide to do a ravenous nosedive into Pranav's hand, I yanked his collar and ordered, "Slugger, off! Now!" The dog smacked his lips and slunk off the bed.

I couldn't help feeling miffed that Pranav had decided to feed him without asking me first. "Bad idea," I said, hearing the edge in my own voice.

Pranav heard it too. "Yeah, I, uh, guess I shouldn't have done that." He set the bag of goldfish on a nearby table while I wiped the pools of dog slobber off the bed.

Don't expect him to know all the ins and outs of proper service dog etiquette. You should cut the guy some slack, the voice inside my head counseled. My words were gentler when I said, "It's the 'no people food' rule; it's really important to follow that."

I invited Slugger back up onto the bed. Pranav petted him and smiled sheepishly at me, "Right, I'm sorry I forgot. I'll remember next time."

Grinning back, I took his hand. "Thanks, that would be great."

Just then, Slugger inched forward. He pushed his big, wet nose between our clasped fingers and rested it there, huffing softly. His gesture was funny and loving. It was also an affirmation: from pretzels to a flying pig, Slugger was part of this, too.

Chapter 10

A Pack of Three

In the days that followed, Pranav and I spent more and more time together. Our affection deepened with every shared smile and tender glance. "I think you're beautiful!" Pranav said. And I believed him. When, at the end of our third date, he leaned in and kissed my mouth lightly, I was surprised, pleased, and somewhat giddy.

"Uh, wow," I stammered as he pulled away. So much for a suave reaction.

Pranav smiled. "That was nice." It was also the first of many kisses we would share. Our physical intimacy deepened as our relationship grew. I felt skittish at first, worried that Pranav might be repulsed by my scarred and unusual body. Two painful experiences back in my earlier years of college had fostered that fear.

One evening when I was a freshman, I'd been trudging toward the campus cafeteria, thinking of the heaping plate of pasta I'd find there. At the time I wasn't considering my unsteady gait or the way it appeared to others. A pack of finely chiseled, rowdy guys approached. They wore lacrosse shirts.

Instinctively, I scuttled to the edge of the rugged walkway. I lacked the nerve to look into the faces of the men's lacrosse team as they passed. Still, I enjoyed glimpses of the *rest* of them. That consolation made me smile. A moment later, one of the athletes erased my grin. He called loudly over his shoulder, "Why do they let those damned cripples in this school anyway?"

I could have said so many things then, if I'd had enough grit, like, "Same reason they let assholes in!" But in that moment I pretended not to hear. I bit my lip; my anger coiled upon itself and snaked into my gut.

That same year I'd noticed three other students with visible disabilities on campus. When I saw them I always felt a strange mix of kinship and self-consciousness. Joe, who was a year ahead of me and used forearm crutches, seemed to sense these emotions.

He approached me in the campus student center one day. I was standing in front of a wall of mailboxes, fiddling with the combination lock of my own slot. He watched for a moment. Then he said, "Has anyone ever told you how sparkly you are?"

Unaccustomed to compliments, I flapped my hand dismissively and turned silly. "That's only because my vitamins have glitter in them."

Joe grinned. We chatted for a while and he asked, "Mind if I come visit you sometime?"

The question caught me off guard. "Oh, well, sure, I guess."

Three evenings later, Joe was sitting on the bed in my dorm room. He was holding my last can of Diet Coke in his left hand, slurping its contents noisily. He complimented everything from my large brown eyes (they resembled a fawn's, he said), to the curve of my butt.

At first I was pleased by his attentions, but before long Joe's flattery seemed as excessive as the cologne in which he'd apparently bathed before visiting. His words made me twitchy, uncomfortable. Still, I thought I should be nice, so I smiled.

Joe returned my grin, but his expression resembled the cocky smirk of a card shark on the verge of playing a trump card. "Come on, baby," he murmured, "you're smart enough to know none of the guys out there want you. Of course they don't; you're a cripple. Thing is, that's no problem for me. I mean I have to use those."

He jerked his left arm up and out, gesturing toward his crutches. Droplets of soda escaped from the can in his hand. They splashed around the raised rim and trickled down the sides. Joe's eyes locked on mine. His tongue flicked out. He pulled its vermillion fatness across the top of the can.

Still staring, he licked the beads of Diet Coke from the edges—slowly. I didn't look at him. I dropped my gaze and curled my sweaty fingers into a ball. Uneasiness tightened my throat; it lifted the delicate hairs at my nape.

After a moment Joe set his drink on my nightstand. "Don't you get it?" His voice sounded gruff as he scooted to the edge of the bed where I sat. Suddenly he threw himself on top of me. I was pinned against the mattress. "Don't you get it?" he said again. "You and me, we're a match. It's a cripple thing."

"Cripple thing, my ass!" I shoved against him with all my strength. He rolled off me awkwardly, grunted.

I was suddenly full of adrenaline and rage. "Get out! Now!"

Joe retrieved his crutches and stood up slowly. Crimson faced, he said, "I didn't know you'd be such a cold bitch. Besides, you can't blame a guy for trying."

"Screw you!" I hissed.

As he moved toward the door, he answered, "That was the whole idea."

The door slammed. I crumpled onto my bed then and held my breath, listening to the steady clicking of retreating crutches.

Now, years after that sound had faded into silence, I was still haunted by the experience. Yet I knew that if I didn't want to be stuck there, if I wanted to move forward, I'd have to do more than face my fear. I'd have to voice it as well.

One night as Pranav and I sat watching TV together, I took a deep breath and said, "I've been wanting to ask you about something. Are you bothered by my disability? I mean it doesn't freak you out in terms of physical stuff—sex and all that—does it?"

Pranav turned his gaze from the small screen, eyes wide with surprise. "What? Why would I . . . " He got up, came over to me, and offered his hand. "Come here a minute." Guiding me to the full-length mirror that hung on the back of my bathroom door, he stood me in front of it. "Look."

But I felt vulnerable, self-conscious now. With a quick laugh, I tilted my head down and to the side. My boyfriend moved behind me. He wrapped his arms around my body. "I mean it. Look," he said softly. I lifted my eyes and as I met my own reflection, Pranav whispered, "That's a warm, sexy, wonderful person. What's not to love?"

His sweet words inspired both my trust and my desire. I turned to embrace him and didn't let go until we'd shared a long and passionate kiss. In the days that followed, Pranav also inspired me to embrace a more wholesome view of sexuality and of myself.

As if sensing this healthy growth, many of my friends smiled when they saw us together on campus. They'd nod to us and then toss a cheerful, "Hey, Sluggie," to Slugger. Still, some acquaintances—those who knew me less well—raised their eyebrows at our cross-cultural romance. Jen, a hall-mate who lived several doors down, approached me one afternoon as I was leaving my dorm.

"Hi, Leigh." Her greeting was friendly, but I heard a note of cautiousness in her voice.

"Howdy," I answered, wondering what was on her mind.

I knew Jen had been born and raised in a small town in North Carolina. She'd mentioned this proudly once as an explanation of her distinctly southern accent. Now she drew her words out, making them slow and twangy. "So that guy you're with a lot now, he doesn't look like he's from round these parts. Where's he from?"

"You mean Pranav." I grinned. "He's originally from India. Why?"

Jen narrowed her eyes, tossed her hair over her shoulder. Her next question soured my mood. "Why in the world would you date outside your race?"

"Well," I snapped, "I've always believed a person's value comes from what's inside his skin rather than by what shade it happens to be on the outside. Now if you'll excuse me, I have to get to class." Jen's mouth formed an astonished *O* that matched her now huge, saucer-like eyes. Poor Slugger had to break into a double-time prance to keep up with me as I brushed past her and out the door.

Though I was adamant in my response to Jen, that didn't mean my relationship with Pranav was free of cultural challenges. I was naively shocked to discover that, while many of my sweetheart's Indian friends had embraced the customs of life in America, some were wholeheartedly against our relationship.

I came face to face with this sentiment one Saturday. We'd been invited to the home of one of

Pranav's classmates for dinner, and I'd been looking forward to it all week. Raj, Pranav's peer, whom I'd met on campus, was soft-spoken and friendly. When his wife, Shoba, welcomed us into their tiny apartment that evening, her gracious demeanor quickly put me at ease.

I'd decided to leave Slugger at home that night, but I thought of him while we all sat 'round the living room chatting. I couldn't help turning my head toward the kitchen every so often just to fill my nose with the savory scents that drifted from the pots on the stove, and I wondered if my nostrils were flaring the way Slugger's often did. As I inhaled glorious whiffs of Indian curry, basmati rice, and spicy lentil dahl, I figured I'd be lucky if I could keep from drooling like him! My mouth was already watering. "Dinner sure smells wonderful, Shoba!"

"Thanks! We'll eat as soon as my folks get here. Should be any minute."

She rose, disappeared into the kitchen, then returned with a tray of crispy, piquant appetizers called *papad*. I was munching on my third piece when her family arrived.

Shoba introduced everyone warmly; still I noticed that her mother kept staring at me. Though strangers often regarded me with inquisitive glances, the expression on the older woman's face did not reflect some semblance of benign curiosity. She glowered unabashedly at me.

How odd! I thought, noting that she was quick to smile at everyone else in the room. Then it hit me: *Maybe she doesn't speak English.* So I nodded to her and ventured a Hindi greeting, "Namaste."

The woman glared, sniffed loudly, and turned her back on me. Feeling suddenly awkward, I tried to catch Pranav's gaze; I knew even a quick meeting of our eyes would offer reassurance. But now Pranav had turned away from me too. He was chatting with Raj. When I reached out to take his hand, he pulled away. *What in the world is going on?* I wondered. Unsure what to say or do, I sat in silence.

Shoba's mother, however, didn't follow suit. She nudged her husband, waggled a long finger at me, and fussed loudly in her native tongue. Though I only knew a few words of Hindi, there was no mistaking her scowling scrutiny. I wondered what in the world made her hateful, when she'd only just met me. I wondered too why no one else seemed to think her behavior was inappropriate. Stealing a quick private moment with Pranav, I whispered in his ear, "Why is Shoba's mom acting so ugly?" Pranav barely acknowledged me; he didn't answer.

The strangeness continued as the evening wore on. Though dinner tasted lovely, I felt increasingly uneasy and out of place, like a last-minute theater understudy called to the stage before I'd even read the script. And Pranav's behavior was more troubling to me than the rudeness I encountered.

Shoba's mother kept up her stream of frowning furor, yet my date offered me no guidance or support. I excused myself as soon as dinner was over, saying I suddenly felt as if I were coming down with a cold. I thanked Raj and Shoba for their hospitality and hurried out the door.

"Want to explain what happened in there?" I said as soon as Pranav and I had climbed into his car. "I didn't want to make a scene in someone else's home, especially after being invited for dinner; but how bizarre, how tacky; that woman was acting ugly toward me all night!"

Pranav wouldn't meet my gaze. "She's just used to speaking her mind."

"Well that's obvious. What was she saying anyway?" I demanded.

After a long silence my date answered hesitantly, "Well, she said you shouldn't be with me. Because you're an American. And she called you a . . ." he paused then said softly, "she said you have loose sexual morals."

Now the confusion and anger I'd felt all evening swelled and pushed the words from my lips, "What? Well if I'd have known that's what she was broadcasting, I would have set her straight!" A moment later a painful realization hit me. "You knew, you *knew* she was calling me an American whore and yet you just sat there calmly eating dinner!"

"I couldn't figure out what to do," Pranav protested meekly.

Feeling furious and betrayed I shot back, "You could've said something. You should have stood up for me!" I took a deep breath and let it out slowly. When I'd calmed down enough to speak without shrieking I added, "If we're going to be a couple, I expect you to support me no matter where we are or who we're with. Don't you get that? Good God, at least my dog does!"

By the time I returned to Slugger a short time later, my anger had turned to hurt. I'd scooted quickly out of Pranav's car the moment we reached the parking lot outside my dorm; when he'd offered to see me to my room, I'd flatly refused. Now I only wanted the sweet, uncomplicated company of my dog. I could hear his tail banging against the furniture in the wag zone as I unlocked my door. I pushed it open, and the eighty-five-pound Lab slipped through the tiny crack with the nimbleness of a door mouse.

"Hey, buddy," I cooed, reaching down to pet my snorting, gyrating companion. "I missed you!" When I stepped into my room, I realized Slugger had missed me too. He had overturned the trash can and pulled out its contents.

Wads of Kleenex and crumpled papers were strewn haphazardly across the floor. An empty lotion bottle perched on its lid in the corner. The Styrofoam clamshell that had held yesterday's dinner was now reduced to millions of tiny tooth-marked pieces.

And squashed in the middle of my lovely, rose-themed area rug was a banana peel. Or at least what remained of it. Slugger had cleaned every single molecule of the sweet fruit from its skin, leaving nothing but a thin, pulpy husk on the scarlet and emerald carpet.

Too drained to get angry again, I closed the door, leaned against it, and slumped to the floor. "Aw, man!" I whined. "As if this evening wasn't a big enough mess already!"

Slugger didn't understand my stress or his part in it, but he seemed to want to help. He promptly came up and licked my cheek. Then he grabbed his stuffed pig and dropped it in my lap as if to say, *Think you might feel better if we played a little?*

"Sorry, Banana-Breath; fun is out of the question until I get all this up." I tossed the toy off my lap and stood up slowly. Fetching a broom and dustpan, I began sweeping up the remnants of the trash raid. Fortunately it was easier to clean up than it looked, and just half an hour later I snatched up a tennis ball and took Slugger outside for a quick game of fetch.

Standing in the cool night air I knew the mess between Pranav and I would take much longer to put right. Still, my partnership with Slugger had taught me the importance of voicing my expectations clearly. And now I'd found the wisdom and self-assurance to do that with Pranav. *If he has a lick of sense, he'll value my opinions and my feelings,* I thought.

After I'd taken a few days to cool off, Pranav showed up at my door, verifying that he did indeed have a lick of sense. He also had an apology and a dozen roses. Though it was clear our relationship held unique challenges, Pranav and I agreed we wanted to try and make a go of it.

The intense discussions and frustrations that marked our next months together confirmed yet another truth I'd first learned from Slugger: relationships—even good ones—can be downright grueling.

With time, understanding, and a commitment to respecting our cultural differences, Pranav and I eventually established a healthy and solid partnership. Along the way we also came upon some of our favorite pastimes. A sort of inter-species rendition of hide-and-seek was at the top of our list. Perhaps that was because Slugger clearly adored playing it with us.

"Look out, look out for the Labrador; he always finds what he's looking for!" Giggles punctuated my sing-song announcement as it echoed through Pranav's apartment during one afternoon game. My role in our funny hide-and-seek sport was to be 'The Distractor.'

I always imagined James Earl Jones pronouncing that title, letting it roll majestically from his tongue like velvet thunder: The Distract-or! But in truth, my part had more to do with fun than majesty.

At the beginning of each game, I'd call Slugger using the soft and syrupy tone he found irresistible. "Oh Slugger, come here, sweet boy!" He'd hurtle toward me, every hair on his body drawn by that summons.

Rumph! A heartbeat later I'd find myself cradling the head of an ecstatically snorting Lab. I'd coo and stroke his ears, capturing his attention just long enough for Pranav to slip away and find a hiding place. This time, Pranav headed for the closet in his back bedroom. He tucked himself into the furthest, darkest corner of that closet. Then he waited. By the time I'd warbled my warning, "Look out, look out for the Labrador!" three times, I knew the human hider would be ready for the canine seeker.

A moment later, Pranav's voice drifted through the air on a stage whisper, "Yoo-hoo, Slugger, bet you can't find me!"

My Lab's ears perked. His nose twitched. Now he

backed away from me, forsaking my attentions for the thrill of the hunt. He careened down the hall so fast it looked as if his butt was trying to out-race his front end. But just when it seemed that feat might actually happen, Slugger slammed on his four-pawed brakes. In the automotive world such an abrupt stop would've been accompanied by an ear-piercing screech; my dog only let out a single huff.

Then he stood for a moment, concentrating. He sniffed the air open-mouthed, making a soft *guff guff guff* sound. I came up behind him. "What say you, SherLab Holmes? Can you solve the latest mystery of the missing man?"

He gave me a cursory glance before trotting into the bedroom. There he cavorted around the bed, the dresser, the nightstand. I watched in utter amazement as he ignored a pair of stinky old flip-flops lying on the floor and plunged into the closet. Slugger's wagging rump conveyed what his nose knew: he was close—very close now! A single victorious woof rang out a moment later. *Found him!*

I laughed, "Okay, now *that* was impressive!" When my favorite guys emerged from the closet together, Pranav seemed to be holding up his end of a typical, post-game conversation. "Yeah, yeah, you found me, but you gotta admit I almost had you snookered that time!"

Slugger snorted.

"I could be wrong," I ventured with a smirk, "but I do believe the dog thinks you're full of it."

My sweetheart guffawed. "Probably right!" Then he knelt down and wrapped his arms around Slugger.

"But you like me anyway, don't you boy?"

The Labrador licked Pranav's cheek; there was no mistaking his agreement.

Since the two of them shared a growing and spirited affection, I wasn't surprised when Pranav winked at me one day a few months later and said, "I've grown so attached to Slugger, I'll just have to find a way to spend more time with him!"

"How would you manage that?" I raised my eyebrows coyly. "We already spend all our spare hours together."

"Well," Pranav grinned at me, then quickly looked away. He wiped his palms on his jeans. Slipping a hand into his pocket, he extracted a small black box and flipped it open. "Would you do me the honor?" The words came out on a hoarse whisper.

I looked at the glittering ring he extended toward me before lifting my gaze to meet his. "Is this . . . are you asking me to marry you?"

Pranav smiled now, kissed my lips softly. "I am."

Suddenly blinking back tears, I answered, "Yes."

My sweetheart held my shaking hand and slid the ring onto my finger. "It's perfect," I whispered over the lump in my throat. Sensing my emotion, Slugger trotted up. He nuzzled against my side. I bent down to show him my left hand then. "Look, Sluggie, it's official. We're a pack of three!"

Chapter 11

Changes

The autumn of 1995 marked great changes in my life. Having married in an intimate ceremony at the end of that summer, Pranav and I now happily settled into our first home together. Our one-bedroom apartment was so small that the eighty-five-pound canine member of our family suddenly seemed more like a wooly mammoth—*a shedding* wooly mammoth.

We joked that the situation helped us get better acquainted with each other and with the heavy old Electrolux we'd inherited from Pranav's bachelor days.

The two of us split our household chores, and one Saturday when it was my turn to wrestle with the vacuum, I grumbled, "I hate this awkward-ass machine!"

"What?" Pranav called from the next room.

"This stupid vacuum is a clunky donkey!" I yelled above its maddening monotone screech. The moniker stuck like the tiny hairs that coated our environment, and after that my husband offered to take on "double clunky donkey duty" to de-fur our carpets and furniture.

In spite of all his good-natured attempts to make light of the problem, I sensed that Pranav was really bothered by it. In addition to vacuuming, he often patted long strips of masking tape along the edges of our upholstery. He'd smooth each piece on meticulously and then yank it off with a vengeance. Although the ritual seemed to offer some stress relief, I wasn't convinced it made much of a dent in the fur.

My spouse eventually came to the same conclusion. One evening he returned from work later than normal. He kissed me, then did his usual "good-to-see-you-again-too" jig with Slugger. Once the two of them had finished cavorting around the living room, Pranav announced, "I stopped off at the store on the way home and picked up something I think you're going to like!"

He knew I'd never outgrown a love of surprises, and I immediately launched into question mode, "What is it? Something fun? When do I get it?"

"Hang on and I'll bring it in." Pranav hustled out the front door, leaving me to ponder the possibilities. I hoped his gift might be romantic or edible. Perhaps, like a good box of chocolates, it would be both!

But when my husband returned a few minutes later, he was carrying something far larger than even the biggest Whitman's Sampler. He panted as he set an enormous cardboard box on the floor.

I gasped. "What the . . . ?"

Sharing my curiosity, Slugger trotted up to the

box and began sniffing around its corners. Pranav swatted him playfully. "Glad you're intrigued, since you inspired the purchase."

I peered more closely at the words and images that adorned the cardboard container. "Hah, you clever man. The clunky donkey can be retired at last!" I exclaimed.

Its successor was far from an ordinary vacuum. It was a red canister shop-vac with a powerful motor, a host of attachments, and a sturdy hose that looked as if it could inhale all the loose dog hair within a 50-mile radius.

Pranav grinned as he pulled it from its box. "Yeah, I figured we needed an upgrade. Think of all the money we'll save on masking tape. Besides, as long as we have Slugger in our lives, we should have a vacuum worthy of his fur!"

"Well said!" I hugged my husband then, grateful for his attitude and flexibility.

Pranav's gift was destined to see us both through more dog fur and more changes than we could ever imagine; yet at the time we were only focused on the immediate transformations taking place in our lives.

In addition to being newlyweds, Pranav and I were both launching our careers; he had recently taken a position as a consultant with an educational software company, and with the ink still fresh on my masters diploma, I began working at a community mental health center not far from home.

Slugger and I were walking across the center's staff parking lot one morning when someone called out, "Hey there, would you mind telling me about your dog?"

I knew the folks in HR had promised to announce the addition of a new employee with a mobility assistance dog. *Did the memo go out?* I wondered. Now I paused and turned to see a woman moving toward me. I noticed she had short black hair and a friendly face. And—*whoa*—her gait was nearly identical to mine. When she reached me she said, "Hi, I'm Maria. I work in the substance abuse unit here. I have CP, and ever since I heard you two would be joining us, I've been thinking about how a service dog might help me."

I grinned, feeling a sudden and unexpected kinship with the woman. "Well, for me this partnership is about balance. Obviously Slugger's trained to assist with my physical balance, and there's more to it than that. I mean, let's face it—CP sucks."

A smile of recognition crossed Maria's lips.

"I'm not saying my dog makes all the pain and frustration magically disappear, but he sure helps to balance it. Slugger is the one good thing to come out of my CP. If the two of us can help you decide whether partnership is right for you, we'd be happy to do that."

"Thanks," Maria said. "That'd be great!"

We decided to meet over lunch a few times so that my new friend could ask questions and get a firsthand look at what it was like to work with a service dog. I gave her a Caring Canine Companions brochure and even took Slugger out of his harness so that she could see his "regular dog" side. By the end of our fourth lunch date, Maria proclaimed, "I'm hooked!"

I sensed then that things had come full circle. Just as Anne Cooper and her dog Caesar had inspired me to pursue my partnership with Slugger, now Slugger and I were a source of motivation for Maria. She decided to apply for a service dog from an out-of-state organization, and not long after that, she took two weeks' leave to undergo training with a canine partner.

When Maria returned, she was accompanied by a tall, poodle-mix named Quincy. He wore a harness like Slugger's and had been taught to do many similar tasks. Still, our two canines couldn't have looked more different; while Slugger was barrel-chested and stocky, Quincy had a long, willowy build.

And, in contrast to my fluffy yellow-coated Lab, he sported tight gray curls over his entire body. These, coupled with the bushy brows above his lively eyes, convinced me Quincy would've made the perfect model for a new addition to Jim Henson's Muppets.

I could easily envision such a character as I sat through a center staff meeting one afternoon just days after Maria and her canine partner returned from their training. They were settled across the room from Slugger and me; and every so often I found myself stealing glances at the new dog lying at Maria's feet.

Quincy positioned himself so that he could keep an eye on Slugger, and his perky expression made me guess he'd love to spring up and have a good old fashioned romp. But the youngster, like all service dogs, had been taught not to play or socialize with other dogs while in harness. Even when the two working canines passed in the hallway, they were expected to keep their on-the-job composure.

Slugger seemed intrigued by the center's newest employee, and sometimes I'd have to issue a stern, "Leave it!" to keep his wiggling, sniffing instincts from taking over when Quincy was nearby.

Still, I couldn't blame Slugger for his fascination with the well-trained young dog, and I had to admit he was incredibly cute. "I swear, Quincy is just delightful!" I told Maria when I met her one morning in the staff lounge.

"Isn't he though? And he's such a sweetheart, too. I mean we both have lots to learn, but he sure is a wonder!" Maria grinned, then turned serious. "And Leigh, remember how you said service dogs provide balance that's more than just physical?"

"Yeah." I smiled.

"You were right." Maria stroked the top of Quincy's head. "This guy offers goodness that goes way beyond what's apparent."

I soon discovered that Maria and I weren't the only ones who appreciated the less obvious benefits of a service dog. The clients with whom I now worked had chronic mental illnesses, and many of them voiced the same realization. Several days a week I assisted them in the vocational unit of a day treatment center.

There, I helped participants obtain part-time jobs and volunteer positions throughout the community. They were quick to point out that this was the perfect fit for me—helping people find work while I was accompanied by a *working* dog!

Yet for many of my clients Slugger was more than a friendly, well-trained animal. He was a symbol of hope. If I ever wondered about his impact at the center, all I had to do was show up and get out of my car. The greeting I'd hear quickly became familiar though it wasn't intended for me.

"G' morning! How's my buddy?" It was Frank, a large, red-haired man who delivered those words. He made a point of being the first to meet us in the parking lot every morning, even when it was cold or rainy.

Frank had a challenging mental illness, and he usually withdrew from other people. Yet he was able—even anxious—to relate to my Labrador. Slugger always responded to him with soulful glances and tail wags; for Frank, that was perfect.

Hoping to make the most of this positive connection, I asked if he'd like some special time with Slugger once a week. Frank's boyish face lit up in a rare smile when he replied quietly, "Yeah, that'd be nice." We agreed to meet next Thursday after lunch.

When that day arrived, Slugger's admirer was the first to greet us as usual. But this time his "G'morning! How's my buddy?" was followed a few moments later by, "We'll visit today?"

"Yes indeed, Frank," I assured him. "You can spend some time with Slugger right after lunch."

"That's good," he answered softly. Then he shuffled into the building.

The morning passed quickly; by the time I'd talked with a young man struggling with his depression and reviewed job search progress with several other clients, it was nearly lunchtime. The atmosphere in the center was purposefully relaxed, and Slugger often dozed under my desk while I put my newly learned counseling skills to use. But now the aroma of Shake' n Bake chicken wafted through the halls. It kept my Labrador awake and made my stomach growl. I was grateful when the center's intercom clicked on and a woman announced cheerily, "Lunch is served!"

She and the other members of the kitchen unit had prepared one of their most popular meals: chicken, baked potatoes, and tossed salad. Now the hallways echoed with the sound of hurrying feet as folks flocked to the dining room. I joined the tail end of the migration with Slugger at my side.

"Here you go, darlin'!" Bernice, a jovial long-time member of the kitchen crew, set a plate in front of me as I took my seat at the end of a long dining table.

"Yum!" I spread a napkin across my lap and grinned.

"Yeah, good today," Bernice answered. Then she bent down and peered at Slugger. "Sorry, none for you, sweet boy. Your mama done told me, no people food." Like most of my clients, she respected the rules regarding my service dog and took pride in following them.

"That's right," I said. "Poor dog; as good as the chicken smells today, I bet he'd love to gobble it up."

"Yeah, but it would make him sick!" Bernice proclaimed. Then she winked and added, "Sick for more!"

Cutting into the huge piece of chicken on my

plate, I laughed. "You're probably right about that!"

Frank was sitting at the other end of the room making short work of his own meal. I caught his eye and smiled. He gave a slight nod. *Will he remember our meeting?* I wondered.

But as soon as lunch was over, I had my answer. I was leaving the dining area when Frank came up behind me. I could smell the Italian dressing he'd poured on his salad when he leaned toward me and said simply, "Okay."

"Hi Frank!" I beamed at him. "How was your lunch?"

"Good."

"Glad you enjoyed it. Don't you think the folks here make the world's best chicken?" I asked, trying in vain to engage him in conversation.

"Yeah."

After a moment I said, "How about we go to the library so you can visit with Slugger a bit like we planned?"

"Yeah."

The smooth soles of Frank's worn-out sneakers made a gentle swooshing sound as he followed Slugger and me down the hall. Reaching the quiet room that held books, spare furniture, and boxes full of seasonal decorations, I settled into an old padded office chair. I told my dog to lie down then I smiled at Frank.

"Okay?" he asked.

"Yes Frank, you can visit with Slugger now."

"Yeah," he squatted down, shifted his weight, and sat down hard on the floor beside my dog. Placing one hand next to Slugger's right front paw, Frank stayed still and quiet at first.

Slugger matched the man's demeanor; only his tail swayed slightly. When Frank saw this gentle wag, he began to talk. His words were slow and soft. "Hey there. I know you like me. I can tell. We're buddies, aren't we? You're a pretty fellow, and you're very smart. You're a really good dog too. Super good. That's why I like you so very much."

Watching, listening, I was amazed. I'd never heard this solitary man in his plaid shirt and stained khaki pants utter more than two or three words at a time. Yet here he was making a mini-speech to Slugger!

That sweet and simple testimonial marked progress. It would eventually lead Frank to engage in short but appropriate conversations with me. Now I marveled that the dog who had helped heal so many of my wounds was gently and wordlessly encouraging Frank to take his own steps toward health.

Slugger made a difference as I worked with other mentally ill adults in the community as well. While many of my clients were able to live independently, they needed assistance with things like socialization, proper dosing of their medications, and shopping.

I traveled across town twice a week to visit a woman named Mary. Pulling up outside her apartment one November morning, I maneuvered my silver Honda Civic into the disabled parking space.

Slugger was settled across the backseat; he twitched his eyebrows when I said, "Okay, bud, sit tight a minute. I'll be back in two shakes." I locked the car and hurried to Mary's apartment.

After a single knock on the orange metal door, I could hear her unlatching the bolts. "I was keeping an eye out for you. I always do that on the days I know you're coming."

"Thanks! It's good to see you, Mary," I said as she ushered me in. A little gray cat with white forepaws scampered up to me then. "And it's nice to see you as well, Bootsie," I added with a laugh.

Mary chuckled too. "Oh, he's been full of himself this morning, running around the apartment like a wild man. I knew he'd come say hi though. He likes you; he knows you're an animal person." She paused, scrunched her lower lip. "Not sure he'd be too fond of your dog though. Speaking of Slugger, you got him in the car?"

"Yep!"

"Well I reckon we better get a move on; don't want to keep him waiting too long. Besides, I've got lots to get at Wal-Mart. Want to get started on my Christmas shopping today if that's okay with you."

"Absolutely. I remember we talked about that during my last visit." I said.

"Oh yeah," Mary wriggled into a green quilted jacket and flipped her long brown ponytail over its raised collar. "All set if you are!" A few stray hairs had escaped their holder. Mary shoved them back with the palm of her hand. "Grr, stupid hair," she fussed as I followed her out the door.

I unlocked my car and Mary greeted Slugger as she slid into the passenger's seat. "Hey, you good dog!"

The Lab's tail thwacked in response.

Mary reached behind her, offering Slugger her hand to sniff. He licked it instead. "I got a kiss!" Mary said with a giggle. "See, he can sense an animal person even when he's working. He's like my Bootsie. Just being around him makes me feel good, you know?"

"I'm glad," I said, smiling. "Slugger does seem to have a knack for that."

"Yes indeed, and it helps that he's also a great shopper."

My service dog proved Mary's words when we reached Wal-Mart. He walked calmly up and down the busy store aisles with me as I helped my client pick out gifts for her family. "See?" she said, pausing to gaze at the Labrador, "Slugger doesn't get all worked up about what's going on around him. He just stays focused and takes everything in stride. I should try to be more like him!"

Mary fumbled to unlatch her purse, then plunged her hand into its depths and pulled out a bright pink wallet. Scowling at it, she added, "But some things just make my brain go crazy crazy."

Knowing that basic money management was a challenge for her, I offered, "Mary, would you like me to help keep an eye on the prices of things so you can be sure to stay within your budget?"

"Whew, thanks," she wiped her hand across her forehead. "That'd be great. If you watch the money, my brain will be cool as a cucumber and I'll relax more. Like Slugger, you know?"

"Sounds great," I said. Together we managed to find a blue ocean-scented candle for Mary's sister, a set of tea towels for her aunt, and some sparkly hair accessories for her little niece.

"I have a few more folks to buy for before Christmas, but this is good start," Mary said. She set her purchases on a table in the store's snack bar and sat down heavily. "Gosh, all that shopping made me hungry. I could use a hot dog. What do you say, Leigh?"

Even with Slugger's steady assistance, trekking through the store had tired my legs. "Sounds great! It'll be nice to sit down for a little bit—my dogs are barking."

"What?" Mary glanced down at my Labrador, then grinned. "Oh, you meant your *feet* dogs, not your real dog!"

She giggled so hard that soon I was laughing too. "Yeah, good old Slugger's not made a peep all day. Now if only my feet dogs behaved that well! Come on, let's get a bite to eat."

We ordered hotdogs and Cokes at the front counter. "Would you mind carrying my drink for me?" I asked.

"Sure, that way you won't spill it," Mary replied. "That's something I like about you," she added a moment later.

"What?"

"You ask for help when you need it."

Touched by this insight, I answered, "Well I guess

I learned to do that with Slugger first and then gradually I started doing it with people too."

Mary peered at me over her hot dog. "Yeah, and now I'm learning from you! You're okay just being who you are. I mean, your legs don't work right, but that doesn't stop you. You get out there with Slugger every day, and you help people like me."

She took a long sip of soda before continuing. "I've had my mental problems for so many years, and sometimes even now I just feel like, 'This is too much, I can't handle my mixed up brain anymore.' But then I stop and think of you and Slugger. I figure if you could find such a great way to handle your problems, maybe I can too. I can try, at least."

I was both surprised and honored by Mary's honest compliment, and though the professional texts I'd studied might have suggested a more complex therapeutic response, I went with the one in my heart. "Thank you, Mary. Thank you very much."

In that moment, it was clear that my incredible canine partner was quietly, steadily, doing more than reshaping my own life. He was inspiring positive changes for others as well. In the same way a pebble dropped on a quiet pond sends ripples far out from itself, Slugger's goodness reached beyond him, beyond me. He touched the lives of Maria, Frank, and Mary. And I knew he would touch more.

Chapter 12

Doing Battle

When I was a little girl, my grandfather, Pop Pop, often told me that every part of life held the promise of something good. Pop Pop said if I believed in that promise hard enough, sooner or later I would find a good thing, even in life's most difficult situations.

That was easy to believe when we spent time together on his farm in Virginia's Shenandoah Valley. His words made sense when it came to newborn kittens in the barn and fresh gifts from the garden, but *not* when it came to my disability. I'd never been able to find anything good about having cerebral palsy.

Then, when Slugger came into my life, I realized something good had found *me*. Steadying my wobbly steps, carrying my belongings, and retrieving things I dropped, he was my constant in a volatile world.

Though I could not trust my own body to do what I wanted it to do, I knew I could depend on my service dog. His was an absolute promise: *I'm here for you no matter what.* That promise brought me strength, courage, and self-confidence. I would need all of those in the summer of 1997.

That year Pranav and I moved to southwest Virginia. He'd been offered a job there, and the position, which included a boost in salary without the travel demands he'd faced as a consultant, was too good to pass up.

While my husband jumped into his new job, I got busy turning the rambling old two-story we'd rented into a home. The previous tenants had left the place anything but clean, so I spent days scrubbing our house from top to bottom. All the while, I longed for our tiny apartment in Harrisonburg, where the greatest challenge to cleanliness had been Slugger's fur.

Scraping monstrous globs of mildew from the bathrooms and vacuuming up everything from used Q-tips to mouse droppings, I couldn't help thinking, *Oh, for the sweet days of dust puppies!* No amount of Labrador hair could come close to the grossness of the things our trusty shop-vac now inhaled.

Though Slugger's role in the moving process might best have been described as 'supervisory,' I was immensely grateful for his presence. As I cleaned and gradually began unpacking our belongings, he kept me company and brought me plenty of laughs.

He also took it upon himself to regularly remind me that no matter what condition the rooms of our house were in, the fenced backyard was perfect for playing fetch.

He'd grab a tennis ball (which had naturally been unpacked as soon as we arrived), prance up to me, then swing his head dramatically in the direction of the back door. Slugger seemed to believe that old adage about too much work without recreation, and it was clear he didn't want me to become dull. What could I do but agree to his requests?

Still, my days of playing fetch and setting up house were numbered; I knew I'd eventually need to find a job. Armed with a freshly updated résumé, letters of recommendation, and more than a little optimism, I scoured help-wanted listings in the local paper and online. I applied to every position for which I thought I might be even remotely qualified. Then I waited. Each time the telephone rang, I'd feel a surge of hope.

Maybe this is someone calling to request an interview! I thought, as I hurried to answer the phone's summons late one afternoon. Lifting the receiver to my ear, I tried to make my greeting sound poised, professional. "Hello?"

"Good afternoon, this is Jim Scott. May I speak with Leigh Brill?"

"Speaking."

"Great!" Mr. Scott's tone was cordial as he told me he was calling in reference to a job for which I'd applied with a local agency serving underprivileged clients. "I was wondering if I might ask you a few questions," he said.

My heart skipped a beat, "That would be fine."

Expecting to be asked about my work experience or perhaps my education, I took a deep breath.

"Well, I noticed in your materials you mentioned having a . . . " he paused. "A service dog?"

"Yes, my certified mobility assistance dog helps me deal with the effects of my physical disability," I said, trying to keep my answer clear and formal.

"What?" Mr. Scott sounded suddenly abrupt. "What do you mean by that?"

Instinctively, I spoke carefully now. "I have congenital cerebral palsy. My dog is specially trained to assist with things I have trouble doing on my own. For example, he helps me keep my balance when I walk. He also carries things for me and picks up items I drop."

After a silence that felt as if it stretched for years, I heard, "Oh. Well, I don't know anything about that."

Unsure how to respond to Mr. Scott's words or the petulant tone with which they'd been delivered, I took another deep, calming breath. "Excuse me, sir?" I said, making a point to keep my voice calm.

"I've only heard of seeing eye dogs. Are you blind?" His words were clipped now, accusatory. He sounded as if he were spitting them at me. Uneasiness coiled in the pit of my stomach.

"No, I am not blind. As I said, I have cerebral palsy, and my dog assists with physical tasks I have trouble doing on my own."

"And you *have* to have your dog with you?" Mr. Scott persisted.

Now the discomfort that had settled in my gut

transformed into anger. Like hot lava, it rose in my chest, then pooled in the back of my throat. I fought to keep it from blackening my response when I said, "Yes, my dog helps me in my home, in public, and in work settings."

"Well, we have to consider risk assessment. The thing we are concerned about here," Mr. Scott stopped speaking. He cleared his throat loudly. "What about fleas?" he blurted.

For a moment I was so surprised I could barely breathe, much less answer the question. Eventually I managed, "Fleas? Did you say fleas?"

"Yes, Ms. Brill. We're a public facility. We can't risk ending up with that sort of problem."

Had I uttered the emotional response that sprang into my mind right then, I would've made a smart-ass comment about the fact that, thanks to regular grooming and care, Slugger had never had a flea in his life, and I hoped they didn't have fleas in their public facility because I wouldn't want to risk one jumping on my dog.

Instead I tried to relegate my emotion to my left hand which now gripped the back of a kitchen chair with white-knuckled fury. Still, my voice betrayed me; it quavered when I spoke. "I am sure there are plenty of public health risks you must be wary of in your facility. But if you are assuming my service dog has fleas, I assure you he does not. Because he works by my side every day, I take his grooming and his health very seriously."

"I'm sure you do," Mr. Scott countered dismissively, "but what about bathroom habits? How do you handle that?"

Wanting to assume he meant Slugger's rather than mine, I said that while in harness my canine partner used the bathroom only when given the command to do so. If he needed an unscheduled potty break, he would give me a signal, nudging my hand to let me know he'd like to go out. *Lord,* I thought, *this is turning into an exercise in service dog education.*

That realization prompted my next words, "Mr. Scott, I know you mentioned you're not familiar with service dogs, but I don't see how my dog's habits relate to the job for which I've applied or my qualifications to fill it."

"Oh, your résumé and references are outstanding," he replied enthusiastically. "In fact, we'd like to have you come in for an interview if you're interested."

"You would?" I asked, now thoroughly confused by the man's dramatic change in demeanor.

"Any chance you might be able to come meet with me and the director of the agency next Tuesday afternoon?"

"Uh, well, yeah, sure, that ought to work," I stammered.

But in the days leading up to that appointment, I questioned my own decision. I fretted and wondered, *What if Mr. Scott asks inappropriate questions about Slugger? Worse, what if his attitude is more than just his—what if the whole agency is clueless about service dogs?*

On the afternoon of my interview, I tried to put those uncertainties out of my mind as I walked down the hall at the agency. Slugger was at my side, calm and focused. His presence lent me confidence.

Just relax, the voice inside me said, *Mr. Scott's ignorant about service dogs, but that doesn't mean our meeting can't go well. Besides, I'm sure he won't worry so much once he actually sees Slugger.*

Unfortunately, my self-coaching proved as fragile as a soap bubble; it popped half way through my interview with Mr. Scott and the director of the agency, Ms. Taylor.

Initially, the director radiated the sort of warmth that made me imagine she was probably someone's favorite great aunt. She told me that she'd worked in the human services field for decades and that she, like Mr. Scott, was impressed with my qualifications. When Ms. Taylor went on to compliment Slugger's good manners and ask how he helped me, I felt encouraged. "Would you mind showing us some of the wonderful things he does?" she said.

Although I found her request unusual for a job interview, I complied. Dropping a pen, I had Slugger retrieve it. Then I had him carry a notebook from one end of the room to the other. "My dog does lots more, but it's a bit challenging to show you everything in a small space," I said, gesturing around the tiny office in which we were settled.

"Certainly. I understand." Ms. Taylor nodded and smiled down at Slugger.

Mr. Scott leaned forward then. "Ms. Brill, we would be happy to get you a mechanical grabber and arrange for your co-workers to carry things for you. I'm sure they would also be able to pick up things you drop when needed."

Now I wondered if Ms. Taylor had asked me to demonstrate my service dog's task work merely so her co-worker could tell me that I didn't really need him. I looked at the man and woman sitting there and felt as if I were on the receiving end of a bizarre good cop, bad cop routine.

It was painfully easy to imagine what it would be like to work without Slugger. Every time I dropped something, every time I needed a file from across the room, every time my legs felt especially weak, I'd have to ask an office mate for help.

A single workday would quickly fill up with a litany of requests: *Could you bring me that set of folders from the cabinet, please? Oh sorry, did you think I meant the green ones? I actually need the brown ones . . . Oops, clumsy me, I just knocked my pen on the floor. Would you mind crawling under my desk to retrieve it? . . . Gosh, I need to go to the ladies' room but I'm feeling pretty wobbly. Who wants to be my human crutch this time?*

This form of accommodation seemed impractical and unproductive to me. I couldn't see it fostering healthy interoffice relations, either. By contrast, the interdependence I shared with Slugger brought independence to my life. Taking a deep breath, I reached down and stroked the top of his head. The familiar softness steadied my nerves.

"Okay, I'm confused," I admitted. "Do you mean to say you're offering me a job? We've not even discussed the position. We've only talked about my dog."

"Well," Mr. Scott drummed his fingers against the arm of his chair, "as I mentioned when we spoke on the phone, we must do risk assessment. You are the most qualified candidate we have for the open position. We'd like to offer it to you. We're just," he said and then paused. "We're trying to find a way for you to come and work for us and leave your dog at home. I mean I've never even heard of your sort of partnership. Are there many of you out there?"

A moment later he added, "We're more than happy to make reasonable accommodations for your condition of course." His mouth contorted into an odd, forced grin.

Suddenly I was so angry and indignant that I wanted to slap that grin off his face. But I knew losing my composure would be unprofessional. It would only make me look bad and upset my sensitive canine companion. So I shoved my emotions to the back of my mind and tried to focus on staying detached. "You mean you are willing to make accommodations so long as those don't include my service dog?" I said quietly.

"Well, yes."

Sitting in the cramped office, I discerned a painful irony. I'd just been told that the dog who did so much to increase my independence was banned from joining me in the culmination of that independence—gainful employment.

My cerebral palsy was a lifelong battle I hadn't chosen; I'd grown up being told how to handle it. But now, as an adult, I had a choice—it was both my right and my responsibility to determine *how* I would fight my own battle. I'd decided to face the challenges of my disability with a service dog at my side.

Having gone to graduate school, obtained my masters and educational specialist degrees, and then worked successfully in the mental health field—all with Slugger's assistance—I could scarcely believe what was happening now.

Thoughts and emotions jumbled in my mind like the pieces of a thousand-count jigsaw puzzle dumped from their box. To make sense of them, I had to focus on the things I knew for sure—the absolutes that framed everything else the way straight-edged pieces bring structure to a puzzle.

I forced myself to speak calmly, "The Americans with Disabilities Act includes service dogs as a *legal and acceptable form of accommodation.* Slugger and I have lived and worked together successfully for years, and I plan to continue doing so. If working for the agency here means working without him, I will not do that."

Ms. Taylor blinked at me and pursed her lips. Mr. Scott took a sudden keen interest in his ink pen; he balanced it between both hands and studied it without glancing in my direction. For a while the only sound in the room was Slugger's soft panting.

Finally I said, "Is there anything else?"

Ms. Taylor smiled, as if grateful for some sort of exit. "Well no, I suppose not." She stood, walked to the door, and nodded in my direction. "It was lovely meeting you both, Leigh and Slugger!" I managed perfunctory good-byes and as I stepped out the door, Ms. Taylor added, "Do think about our offer and let us know your decision."

I was so angry now I didn't trust myself to answer.

Later that evening I filled Pranav's ears with my emotions and frustrations. "What the hell?" I fussed as the two of us sipped wine on the couch after dinner. "I have to deal with my CP—with the constant pain, the physical limitations, the lack of control. Shouldn't I at least have the right to determine how I'll manage all that? It's not like Slugger's a water buffalo—he's a legal form of assistance—a very well-behaved, clean and helpful one!"

My breath caught. "He's so much more than that, too. He's the balance to all the hard stuff, the one good thing to come out of my disability. I won't give that up. I won't!" Tears streaked down my cheek then and speckled my shirt.

"Oh, honey," Pranav said as he wrapped his arms around me, "What can I do to help?"

I sniffed. "I'll be okay. I just need to cry."

But before long I realized it would take more than tears to set things right. A few days after my disturbing interview, I phoned the agency. When I asked to speak to Ms. Taylor, I was transferred to her voicemail.

Grateful for the chance to leave a clear and uninterrupted message, I confirmed that I'd given some thought to our recent conversation. I spoke carefully when I added, "My position on this issue remains the same as when we met: I am not interested in any job which does not allow me to be accompanied by my certified service dog. If, however, you would like to discuss the possibility of my working for the agency with his assistance, please let me know." I left my phone number then, clinging to the hope that I'd soon get a phone call.

That call never came.

I knew I could choose to put the whole experience behind me, chalk it up to other people's ignorance, and move on. Part of me wanted to do that. But another part, something deep within me, whispered, *Make things right.*

At this point I knew making things right wouldn't include working for the agency; I wouldn't dare take a job with them after my experience. Still, two questions haunted me: How could I *not* stand up for my right to work with the dog who had changed my life? And if I didn't stand up, what would happen to the next service dog partner who sought a job with the agency?

I shared those powerful questions with Pranav late one night. We'd been discussing this issue for hours, and now *what ifs* dashed round and round my mind like crazed kittens in a game of chase: What if I decided to take some formal action against the agency?

What if my efforts ended up hurting instead of helping? What if they made things bad for other service dog teams? What if they made things hard for me and for my family? My husband and I hadn't even been married very long. We'd lived in our new home for less than a year.

Grasping Pranav's hand, I whispered as tears of fear and frustration slid down my cheek, "I must be crazy for even thinking about fighting this. It's such a huge risk. I'm not sure I have the strength for it. I'm not even sure *how* to fight it."

"Well I don't think you're crazy at all," my husband's voice was as soft and soothing as a favorite blanket. "If there's anything worth taking a risk for, it's your incredible bond with Slugger."

Pranav wiped a tear from my face and gazed into my eyes. "Even though you may not always feel it, you are a strong, strong person. I know you, Leigh; if you choose to fight this, you'll find the strength to fight it well. Whatever you decide, I'm in your court. Sluggie and I are with you 110 percent!"

"Really?" I said. "Thanks. That makes all the difference."

Strengthened by Pranav's adamant support, I contacted my friend Amy for help the very next day. Amy was a dedicated volunteer with Caring Canine Companions, and she also worked as a paralegal. When she heard my story, she suggested I speak to Thomas Oxenham, with the Chandler Law Group.

Initially the very idea of taking any sort of legal action filled me with uncertainty. I'd never even thought of doing anything like this before. And though my partnership training with Slugger had familiarized me with the basics of the Americans with Disabilities Act, I knew nothing about the legal process.

Thankfully, Mr. Oxenham was patient and helpful during our first meeting. He listened attentively as I recounted my experience. Then he explained my options and what I might encounter if I chose to move forward.

Having internalized the societal stereotype of the sweet, compliant southern girl, I felt a sting of guilt even as I sat talking to the lawyer. My tone was muted, apologetic when I said, "It's just that I believe that people who use service dogs should have the same opportunities as those who do not. Isn't that reasonable?"

"Yes, Ms. Brill, that's absolutely reasonable." Mr. Oxenham's next words held a quiet intensity. "And it's also the law."

Then I knew—with this man's professional guidance, and Pranav and Slugger by my side, I could act on my conviction.

I began by filing a complaint with the Equal Employment Opportunity Commission (EEOC). My lawyer had given me a heads-up: the commission's work would be lengthy and involved. So I submitted the exhaustive documentation required for a claim and settled in to wait.

The EEOC investigator handling my case phoned with regular updates over the next several months. Still, time seemed to drag on. Summer's sweltering days slowly yielded to crisp autumn afternoons and the same question sat unanswered in my mind: *Would the EEOC rule in my favor?*

Finally, finally, I received the phone call I'd been both dreading and longing for. The EEOC investigator's voice was familiar and professional. "The commission has reached a determination," she said.

Now I was too nervous to utter a coherent sentence. "Uh, okay."

"Ms. Brill, the EEOC has determined reasonable cause to believe that the agency has violated the terms of the Americans with Disabilities Act in your case."

"They did? I mean, you did? I mean, oh gosh, thank you. Thank you so much!"

"You're welcome, Ms. Brill. We'll be sending you a letter of determination that outlines our findings and our suggested course of action. A copy will go to the agency as well. If you have any questions once you've reviewed your letter, please don't hesitate to contact me."

"Sure, okay," I answered, feeling giddier than I had in a long time.

That elation, however, was short-lived. While the letter of determination offered validation, the commission was unable to reach a suitable conciliation with the agency regarding my complaint.

So, in the summer of 1998, Mr. Oxenham filed a suit in court on my behalf. More than anything, I wanted assurance that the agency would not discriminate against people with service dogs in the future. I didn't want a job with them; I didn't want their money.

Why, I wondered naïvely, couldn't they just say, "We messed up. We shouldn't have said you couldn't bring your service dog to work here. We're sorry and we are now taking steps to avoid repeating our mistake." For me, that would have been enough.

I said this many times. I even suggested resources for learning about service dogs and the access rights of people partnered with them.

But my efforts to increase awareness seemed to fall flat. The legal process continued for months, and even with Mr. Oxenham's caring and expert guidance, the stress was taking its toll. I wasn't sleeping well and was becoming increasingly irritable.

Pranav, who was often the hapless target of my grouchiness, suffered from frequent, debilitating headaches. So we were both relieved when, shortly after a summary judgment in the case, the attorney for the agency contacted my lawyer to say they would like to settle out of court.

On the afternoon when we met to sign that agreement, I felt exhausted. I also feared what could happen to my fledgling family—and our finances—if we ended up losing this case.

Yet at the same time, I wanted—I needed—to know my efforts had mattered. I tried mightily to include a requirement of service dog access education for all agency employees as part of our final settlement, but the agency's lawyer flatly refused. "That," he said, "would be been an admission of guilt. And we have done nothing wrong."

The lawyer's words, at the end of this long and painful battle, deflated me. For a moment I felt as if the conviction on which I'd stood for months was melting like snow in sunshine. Had it all been worth it? I wasn't sure. Swallowing hard to keep from crying, I stared at the floor.

Just then Mr. Oxenham leaned over to me. He put his hand on my shoulder and whispered, "You hold your head up, Leigh! There's honor in doing what's right. You did the right thing in all of this, and because you did, the agency won't make the same mistake again. I feel sure of it."

My lawyer's words stayed with me long after the

bitterness of my fight faded into memory. They echoed in my mind with particular sweetness one evening years later. I was flipping through the TV channels when a segment on the local news caught my attention. It concerned the same agency with which I'd fought my legal battle.

"Talk about working like a dog," the reporter announced cheerily at the start of the story. A smile of amazement crossed my lips as the feature unfolded. It was about a long-time agency employee, Erin Richards. And her new service dog, Ash.

Chapter 13

Heart

Several months later, the sound of familiar footsteps interrupted my workday focus. I looked up from the papers piled on my desk at the Ronald McDonald House of Southwest Virginia to see Julie, a young cancer patient and houseguest, standing in her robe and pajamas.

"Hey! Thought I'd come find you," she said. "Can I hang out with Slugger on his next break?"

"Sure," I answered. "How 'bout right after lunch?"

"Aw man!" Julie's face fell. She ran the fingers of her left hand over her chemo-smoothed scalp. "I gotta be back at the hospital at 12:30, but I really, really, reeeeally need a Slugger visit."

"Hmm," I nodded. The wheels of my office chair squeaked softly as I scooted away from my desk. Slugger was curled at my feet. I sometimes slipped him out of harness so that he could bring some canine comfort to houseguests who needed him; Julie was one of his favorites.

Now the Lab peered up at me with huge, pleading eyes. The look on his face matched the expression of his young friend, *Please?*

My job as the communications director here had proven perfect; in addition to helping me put my experience of discrimination behind me, it was fun and extremely rewarding.

People like Julie were the reason why. Though I needed to put the finishing touches on the latest edition of the house newsletter that was scheduled for mailing next week, I knew it could wait.

What sort of communicator could I claim to be if I didn't get the immediate message in my office loud and clear? Bending down to unfasten Slugger's harness, I said, "Reckon there's nothing wrong with a quick break now."

"You're the coolest!" Julie exclaimed. This was quite a compliment, since *cool* seemed to be her favorite word. She scampered over and plopped onto the floor.

I gave Slugger his "go say hi" command. Knowing this meant he was free to visit, he shook himself and grabbed the end of his leash in his mouth. Julie laughed with delight when the big Lab promptly stretched out across her lap.

"Think that means you want a belly rub, huh, buddy?" She buried her hands in his coat, moving her fingers rhythmically so that the sparkly blue polish on her nails flashed against my dog's yellow fur. Slugger's tail beat the floor. He sighed contentedly. Before long his tongue lolled out the side of his mouth.

"You big, goofy lug," Julie murmured as she

massaged his neck.

I grinned. "You're putting my dog in a state of bliss."

Looking down at the relaxed and smiling girl now cradling the Labrador, it was clear that joy was mutual. "Cool," she said, "that's cool." After a while she roused Slugger from his trance and stood up.

"It seems Slugger thought your outfit needed a little yellow added in," I observed.

Julie carefully plucked two dog hairs from her sleeve. Then she stopped. Her face lit up in a mischievous grin. "Actually, he's right! I'll leave the rest."

"Well if you ask me, dog fur makes a wonderful fashion statement," I winked.

Julie wrapped her arms around my neck then and planted a quick kiss on my cheek. "This is kinda my escape. When I'm with you guys, I don't have to think a lot or worry—I can just be regular old me. That's cool, you know?"

"It's cool for us, too," I answered. "Sluggie and I love hanging out with regular old you!"

As I watched Julie slip back through the door of my office, I realized that the warmth my dog had shared with her offered a simple affirmation. Even when he wasn't in work mode, Slugger's heart-to-heart message was clear: *You are more than pain, more than worry, more than cancer. You are you. And you are good.*

It wasn't just patients who were reassured by Slugger's presence at Ronald House. He touched the family members with whom I worked, too. Weary parents and grandparents often trudged through the front door of the house after spending long hours at a child's bedside in the hospital.

Many times they simply wanted to be left alone. They'd nod wordlessly then and retreat to the sanctuary of their private rooms. Other times these family members needed to talk, to fill another person's ears with detailed updates on a loved one's condition.

But there were also days when the ears most sought after weren't human; sometimes only Slugger's would do. Then I'd slip the dog's harness off and try to stay out of the way as he provided his unspoken and unconditional solace.

"We have a dog at home called Benny, but he's much smaller than you and not so well behaved," Andrea, a young mother, told Slugger late one afternoon as she stroked his back gently during one of his work breaks. She and her family were well known at Ronald House; her little boy Ryan had been diagnosed with a brain tumor and was a patient at the nearby cancer center.

Andrea had recently told me he was undergoing aggressive treatment. "He'll make it though," she'd added. "Ryan's tough. He comes from hearty folks!" The resolve had sounded strong in the mother's voice then, different from her tone as she whispered to Slugger this afternoon.

Now her words were soft, almost tentative. "Ryan

misses his dog something awful, you know. He just adores Benny. He's always had a soft spot for any kind of animal, ever since he was tiny; that's just the kind of kid he is. I know he'd love you, Slugger. I told him all about you."

Andrea's voice trembled as she continued, "I've promised him when he's better I'll bring him over here to the house so he can meet you. He'll get a real kick out of that. When he's better. What do you say? And in the meantime I'll give you two hugs—one for me and one for Ryan."

Slugger stayed still and quiet as Andrea bent and embraced him. Twice she wrapped her arms around the big Lab and held on. After her long second hug, she stood up. "Thank you," she murmured without meeting my gaze.

"Anytime, Andrea." Part of me wanted to say more, to offer some hopeful or supportive words; but I held my tongue as the woman moved past me and down the hall toward her room. She had just let her guard down with Slugger in a way I'd seldom seen her do with other people.

However briefly, Andrea was able to let go of the roles of the strong mother, the caretaker, and the appreciative houseguest. She'd simply allowed herself to be in the moment, to need and to receive comfort. There was more healing in that than any words could impart.

Now I smoothed the damp spots in Slugger's coat where Andrea's tears had fallen. "Hey, sweet dog," I said, carefully strapping his harness in place once more. That harness was an outward symbol of a dedicated and well-trained service animal.

Yet as I'd watched Slugger with Andrea, I'd been reminded that his most remarkable quality didn't come from his work uniform or all his training— whether in harness or off duty, Slugger offered his heart freely.

Days later, Slugger proved this in an even more powerful and unexpected way. It was 7:30 in the morning, and having seen Pranav off to work, I headed into our tiny downstairs bathroom to get a shower.

Slugger knew better than to try and squeeze his sizeable self into the cramped space between the tub and the door. As had become his habit, he positioned himself across the threshold. The big Lab laid flat on his belly there with his head between his outstretched front paws and his back legs flipped out behind him. He looked as if the only thing he needed to take flight was a flashy cape. "Su-per dog!" I laughed and stepped into the tub.

Slugger was still at his post by the time I finished my shower and put on my bathrobe. I was wringing water from my hair when he suddenly stood up, looked down the hallway, and raised his ears.

Just as I was about to ask him what was up, an odd noise reached my own ears. Unable to decipher it, I froze and listened hard. The noise was coming from the kitchen.

At first I thought, *I bet it's a mouse. Heaven knows we've seen plenty of those since moving into this drafty old house!* But then the sound came again. And this time the persistent rattling banished all thoughts of pesky scampering rodents. Someone was shaking the knob of the door that led from the screened porch into the kitchen. *Oh God,* I thought, *Please let the lock hold!*

Slugger stayed by my side when I dashed into the nearest bedroom. The dog's hackles were raised, and as I grabbed the phone to call the police, I heard his low growl. Then I heard something else—the soft squeak of the kitchen door being pushed open. *Oh crap!*

The floor creaked as the intruder moved across its tired panels. Frantically I dialed 911. The dispatcher's voice was calm, "911, what's your emergency?"

I blurted my address breathlessly into the receiver and kept talking as fast as I could, "My house is being broken into. I'm alone, I mean it's just me and my dog. I need help. Send a car over here fast!" But it was too late; when I looked up, I saw someone standing in the hallway just beyond the bedroom door.

Slugger saw him too; a rumble poured from Slugger's throat then. He stood directly in front of me, staring at the intruder with his hackles raised. And for once, Slugger's tail was completely still. I'd never before witnessed this side of my usually docile dog, but I knew beyond a doubt he was serious about protecting me now.

That knowledge gave me courage. I grabbed the sharpest thing I could find, a silver letter opener, and pointed it at the lanky, scraggly-haired teenage boy who was standing in the hallway gawking at me and my dog. "I don't know who you are, but you better get the hell out of my house! The police are on their way!" I yelled. I tried to sound fierce, especially since I was certain my robe-clad, letter-opener-wielding appearance was far from intimidating.

But Slugger was intimidating enough for both of us. He kept up his steady growl as he glared at the stranger in the hallway. Though the dog remained perfectly still in front of me, the intruder seemed convinced my big Lab might lunge for him any minute.

His glazed and bloodshot eyes kept flitting nervously in Slugger's direction and he wiped his hands repeatedly on his jeans. Finally he spoke. His speech seemed fragmented, as if words were floating haphazardly from his brain to his lips.

"Uh, a friend of mine, you know, what's-her-name," he paused, "Amanda, she's not here anymore?" Another long pause. "I just came by to get some . . . you know, some *stuff* from her."

He gave Slugger a long sideways look and added, "That dog *really* doesn't like me. I don't want any . . . any trouble with him. So if you'll keep him from coming after me, I'll just go now." Then he backed away quickly, not daring to turn his back on Slugger until he'd reached the porch. A distinct smell hung in his wake; it conjured up visions of skunks in burnt clover.

By the time the police arrived, I'd changed into jeans and a T-shirt and was sitting on the couch with Slugger stretched out beside me. He was rarely allowed on the furniture, but after our ordeal I wanted to be as close to my big dog as possible. I couldn't seem to stop hugging him.

Apparently aware that the morning's havoc was past, Slugger was now back to his friendly, happy self. When I ushered the young police officer through the front door, Slugger gave his shoes a thorough sniffing. His tail, I noticed, had resumed its familiar wag.

"What a great dog." The officer smiled.

"*Great's* an understatement," I said. "*Hero's* more like it!" With that, I launched into a detailed account of my scary and bizarre morning, describing the intruder as accurately as I could. "And Slugger here, he's been my service dog for years, and he wasn't about to let that weird guy get near me," I added. "He guarded me the whole time. And he gave the dude a good fright in the process!"

"Quite a partner you've got there," the policeman said warmly. Then he turned sober. "I'm sorry to have to tell you, but your home has a bit of a rough history. Sounds like it caught up with you today."

I gasped as he went on to say that the previous tenants of the house had been very involved in the local drug scene. They'd been known to host a constant stream of "friends," many of whom had been given spare keys so that transactions could happen any time of the day or night.

I was beginning to put two and two together. "That explains the 'stuff' the guy was after, and how he got in. No wonder he smelled strange and acted so freaky!"

"Yeah," the officer answered. He checked the

house inside and out, and when he'd finished he advised, "Looks like everything's fine now, but to be safe you should change all the locks in this place right away. We'll send extra patrols around your neighborhood for the next couple of days to keep an eye on things as well."

I nodded and thanked the policeman, vowing to follow his guidance. As he left, he added, "Oh, and if I were you, I would keep Slugger with me at all times; there's just no substitute for a well-trained dog!"

"I sure will!"

It wasn't until the police cruiser had pulled away from the curb that I realized the officer had mistakenly believed Slugger's protectiveness was a trained response. While there was no denying my dog had been taught many helpful and impressive things, protection wasn't one of them. Such selflessness didn't come from his training. Like his gifts of unconditional comfort and affirmation, it came from his heart.

Chapter 14

Milk-Bones in Lemonade

The sensation came to me slowly at first, seeping around the edges of my consciousness until it had soaked through to my awareness. Now there was no denying it—my ear hurt!

The thin, curled cartilage of its outer ridge felt as if it were burning. *Gosh*, I thought, *talking on the phone doesn't usually hurt. How strange! We've only been chatting for . . .* I glanced at the clock. *What? No way!* The bright red numbers on its digital face showed 9:47 p.m. I'd had the receiver pressed against my ear for more than three hours—suddenly the pain made sense.

It was hard to believe that this marathon chat was also my very first conversation with Carol Willoughby. Prior to calling her, all I knew about Carol was that she had just co-founded a nonprofit service dog organization.

A Ronald House volunteer who'd been friends with her for years had passed along Carol's phone number saying, "I bet the two of you will really hit it off!" Now, with the evening teetering on the edge of ten o'clock, I realized that prediction had proven to be an understatement.

Naturally Carol and I spent quite a bit of time talking about our dogs. She listened empathetically as I gushed about Slugger, and I felt an immediate connection to her as she talked of Booker and Blake, her Golden Retrievers.

Booker, Carol's first service dog, had passed away recently, but while by her side he'd helped her deal with the challenges of rheumatoid arthritis. He'd gone on to assist with the training his young protégé, Blake, and was the inspiration behind Carol's decision to form Saint Francis Service Dogs.

A few months after that first long-winded conversation, I exclaimed, "I can't imagine starting a foundation the way you did, Carol!" The two of us were relaxing on her patio, sipping pink lemonade and eating Cheetos on a pleasant April afternoon.

"Oh you could *too* imagine it." Carol grinned impishly and referred to one of our many inside jokes: "All you'd have to do is take a shower!"

I'd been cradling my glass in my hand, but her words made me laugh so hard I had to set it down quickly to avoid dousing myself in lemonade. Not long ago, I'd told Carol of my decision to send some of my short stories out to magazines to see if I could get them published. When she'd been kind enough to be my "first ears," listening as I read them and offering suggestions, I confided that my cure for writer's block was often a hot shower. "Somehow that just gets my creativity unstuck," I'd told her.

After that, she'd advise me to take a shower any

time imagination was called for. Now she said, "Wouldn't people think we were nuts if they heard the way we talk?"

Looking at the attractive woman sitting in her teal motorized wheelchair, I nodded. Today, as always, she exuded an air of classiness that went far beyond her stylish outfit, polished nails, and spiffy spring hat. Yet I was privileged to know her zany side, too.

Carol and I had quickly recognized we shared something even deeper than disabilities and service dogs. From the start, our friendship never felt new— it felt as if we were simply picking up where we'd left off. In our goofier, dog-obsessed moments, we often joked that we must have been littermates in an earlier life. The thought always made me smile.

Now I popped a Cheeto into my mouth and turned thoughtful. "You know, Carol," I said, wiping bright orange residue from my fingertips, "I've just realized something."

"Uh-oh! Do I dare ask?" she teased.

"Well, it just hit me—you have Milk-bones in your lemonade!"

"What?" Carol shrieked. Her wide-eyed gaze flew to the nearby table where a glass pitcher held ice cubes bobbing in a sweet pink bath.

"I don't mean for *real*. It's that old saying—you know, when life gives you lemons. You figured out how to make something positive from your own struggle. Then you took it a step further when you decided to start your service dog foundation. Ta-da! Milk-bones in your lemonade!"

"Oh, I get it. For a minute there you had me

worried," Carol laughed. "But I didn't do it alone. I couldn't have started any of this without the support of my husband, Doug. And there are so many other folks too, people who believe in the cause and want to help. You ought to know that!"

Recalling how easily my charismatic friend had convinced me to join several foundation committees to help with everything from fund-raising and event planning, to candidate screening, I grinned. "Good point."

"So, Leigh, that reminds me, there's something I need to ask you."

"Shoot," I said, fully expecting I was about to be asked to serve on another committee.

"Our board of directors needs to expand, and well, I was wondering if you—you and Slugger— would join us."

Carol's words caught me off guard, and I suddenly felt unqualified and self-conscious. "Me? Really? Are you sure? I haven't lived around these parts long. I'm not even thirty yet. I mean I'm not sure I can offer much in the way of . . ."

"Stop that!" my friend's exclamation cut into my inventory of insecurities. "How can you say you wouldn't have much to offer? You're smart, you're well spoken, and you have a service dog, so you understand the foundation's mission from the inside out. Our board needs that perspective. We need you!" Then she added the clincher. "It would mean so much to me. Will you give it some thought?"

"Absolutely," I promised. In truth I was pretty sure I'd accept nomination to the board even before our visit ended. I just wanted a few days to think it over. When I called Carol later in the week to officially inform her of my decision, neither of us realized it would mark the start of more than a decade of service!

On the board I saw firsthand what volunteers could accomplish. Dog trainers, puppy raisers, lawyers, veterinarians, entrepreneurs, teachers—people from every walk of life—teamed up. These folks, who were strangers to me at first, valued not just highly trained assistance dogs, but also the people whose lives they enriched.

Our common goal was to raise dogs, raise awareness, and raise funds to improve the lives of others through service dog partnership. Being part of something so much bigger than myself brought me personal validation. It also brought a new sense of purpose to my life.

Shortly after joining the board, I began doing educational talks and demonstrations with Slugger on behalf of the foundation. Civic, church, and school groups often requested these service dog awareness presentations. I'd make a detailed outline before each one, tailoring my points to fit the age and size of every new audience. Though I wasn't immune to stage fright as I addressed groups of curious strangers, Slugger's presence and eager assistance boosted my confidence.

Eventually, I told Carol, "I had no idea I'd end up enjoying awareness presentations so much, but I confess they've become one of my favorite ways to support the foundation!"

My friend winked, "You're great! And the more of those you do, the more Milk-bones we'll be able to add to our lemonade!"

I'd lost count of just how many presentations Slugger and I had done by the time we hurried across the parking lot of a local elementary school several months later. I looked to my canine partner and asked, "Ready to do it again, Slugger?" The jaunty wag of his tail conveyed *All set!*

Even as he grew older, Slugger loved doing ability awareness presentations. They allowed him to show off his service tasks, and he knew he'd be rewarded with cheers and cheese treats.

For me, these presentations provided a chance to share a positive message about service dogs and people partnered with them. While educating young, naturally curious audiences, I often discovered my own rewards of healing and empowerment.

Today was no exception. Having entered the school auditorium full of four hundred wiggly, energetic kids, my companion was standing beside me—just standing there—and *bam;* he captured the attention of every single child. It was an impressive feat. Especially for a dog.

The children packed into the auditorium understood there was something very special about my eighty-five-pound yellow Labrador. They gazed at him with wide-eyed fascination. A cute girl ran the fingers of one hand over the ridges of her braided pigtail. Then she lifted her other hand and pointed to the harness the dog was wearing. She called out, "What's that for? Is that a blind dog?"

I smiled to myself and thought, *Hopefully Slugger and I will make this memorable so she'll learn the answer now and take it with her when she's an adult in the working world! Maybe then, future service dog teams won't face the discrimination we've experienced.*

"Brittany, just wait," a nearby teacher admonished. "Ms. Brill is going to talk to us in a minute; first we have to remember our manners and be good listeners."

She and her co-workers moved among the students issuing similar reminders. Their hushes and shushes floated over the hubbub as my canine companion and I approached the front of the room.

Four stairs led up to the stage there. The two of us started up them in our usual fashion. Slugger moved ahead of me, placing his front paws on the step in front of him. Then he stood perfectly still.

I gripped the rigid handle of his harness, ready to follow him. But suddenly, as I tried to go up the step, my hand slipped. For a terrifying moment my balance vanished. Instinctively I grabbed whatever I could find. My fingers latched on to one of Slugger's harness straps and I stumbled into him. The faithful dog yelped in pain, but he didn't move. He held his position until I'd regained my footing.

Once we'd cleared the stairs, I bent down and checked on him. "My God, are you okay, sweet boy? I'm so sorry I fell into you like that!" I said softly. Guilt reddened my face until Slugger promptly turned his head and gave my nose a quick lick. Perhaps that was his way of communicating, *No harm done.* Or maybe his message was more profound: *It's part of our deal. I'm here for you. No matter what.*

By the time the two of us reached center stage and I'd taken a seat, the chatter in the room had been replaced by astonished whispers: "Wow! Did you see that? How'd that dog learn to do that? I wish my dog was that smart!"

Slugger relished the appreciation; he wagged his entire back end. His gaze darted from me to our audience and back again. He was anxious to demonstrate his skills. Still, introductions had to come first.

Looking out at the sea of expectant faces before me, I felt suddenly awkward. Though public speaking had become such a familiar part of my life now, those emotions still haunted me. They'd been as much a part of my childhood as my imaginary friends, Jiffy and Piggy; yet unlike my make-believe playmates, they'd grown out of reality. Doctors, nurses, peers, and strangers had so often disparaged my body and movements that I'd developed a profound fear of being watched. But now I reminded myself that those experiences, like Jiffy and Piggy, belonged in the past.

Come on, the voice inside me coaxed, *let go of the stage fright. The sooner you relax, the sooner the fear will leave.* I smiled first at my audience, then at my dog. I gave him the down command and began. "Hi everyone! It's great to see you all today. My name is Leigh, and this is my partner, Slugger."

At the mention of his name, Slugger lifted his ears, cocked his head to the side, and stared at me. I gave him a quick grin before continuing. "Slugger's excited to be here, and he has some very important things to show you. You see he's not a regular pet. Slugger is a service dog. That's why he's wearing all this." I paused, extended my left arm, turned my hand palm up, and raised it.

Seeing the nonverbal command, Slugger jumped to his feet. He stood motionless while I pointed out and explained different parts of his working outfit—the vest with the "Please Do Not Pet" patches, the zippered side pouches, and the brown leather walking harness.

"Just like a policeman wears a hat and blue suit to help people recognize him, a service dog wears this uniform so that you'll know he's working," I said.

I gestured for Slugger to lie down once more. Then I announced, "I have an illness called cerebral palsy. My legs and hands don't work like other people's do, so I have trouble doing some things."

It was Slugger who first gave me the confidence to speak these truths without blushing. Such self-assurance was one of many benefits to come from our partnership. For me it proved to be as important and as powerful as the physical assistance Slugger provided.

Still, the observable tasks were impressive, and my young spectators were restless now. I adopted a chummy tone. "You know, everyone faces challenges. All of us in here have things that are hard or frustrating in our lives, don't we?"

"Math homework!" a little boy called out.

A girl with red glasses piped up, "Pop quizzes!"

"My baby brother!" another shouted. "He's two years old and a pain!"

"Great examples," I said, "And I'll let you in on a secret. Sometimes when my body won't do what I want it to do, I feel really, really mad." I twisted my face into a goofy mock scowl until giggles popped through the audience. "The trick—the real trick—to beating any challenge is finding a creative way to handle it. That's why Slugger is here. Let's see if he's ready to show you." I reached down and patted my dog. "Ready, boy?"

After years of working with me, Slugger recognized the word *ready*. He stared at me with shining eyes, waiting. The instant I tapped the fingers of my right hand to my thumb, conveying the signal for *bark,* he obeyed.

His deep voice resonated across the auditorium and bounced off the brightly colored rows of student artwork adorning the walls. Quietness was prized in this place, and Slugger's noisy obedience generated both astonishment and glee.

"Whoa!" one youngster exclaimed. He tossed his head back and gazed at the ceiling as if Slugger's bark might have left a visible trail there the way an airplane draws a line across the sky.

"Awwww, he barked," a cherub-faced girl said to her classmate. I could imagine her using the same tattling tone to report peers who cut in line or forgot to push in their desk chairs.

I held up my hand. "Okay, folks, listen up. I know it's unusual to have a big barking dog in school. But Slugger is trained to bark on command for a reason. If I'm alone and I need help from another person, I tell Slugger to bark until someone comes to see if I'm okay. He responds to both hand signals and word commands so that I can get help when I need it.

"I bet you've already figured out that service dogs like Slugger have to be very smart. In fact, Slugger went to school for two years. First he had to master basic things like *come,* and *sit,* and *heel,* and *stay.* After that, his trainer, Vickie, taught him special service tasks."

I took a deep breath and went on. "Because of my CP, I drop stuff a lot. It's also hard for me to bend down and pick up things. Slugger solves those problems for me."

To demonstrate, I pulled a pen from my skirt pocket and held it up. "This is really little, so it may be hard to see, especially for folks in the back of the room. Is there someone with really sharp eyesight up front here who can let everyone know what I've got in my hand?"

A little girl in the first row chirped, "It's an ink pen!"

"Thank you, Eagle Eye." I dropped the pen and then instructed Slugger to retrieve it. Our young audience watched in spellbound silence as Slugger spit the rescued pen into my hand. I held it up once more and they burst into wild cheers.

"Don't you think my partner deserves a reward for his hard work?" I asked.

The children's response was unanimous and enthusiastic: "Yes!"

I unzipped the outer compartment of my leather purse and extracted a piece of string cheese. Peeling back its plastic wrapper, I broke off a bite-sized chunk. "Slugger, sit." My dog's hind end dropped immediately to the floor. His tail swished and bubbles of drool collected at the corners of his mouth.

I addressed my audience once more. "What are some of your favorite foods?"

"Pizza with extra cheese!" someone shouted.

"Hamburgers!"

"Chocolate ice cream!"

"Wow, you're making me hungry!" I teased. "Well, Slugger's favorite food is cheese. He loves any kind—cheddar, Swiss, sandwich cheese, you name it. I'm giving him a bite now to let him know he completed that hard task successfully."

I slipped the morsel into the palm of my hand and offered it to Slugger. He took it with a single sloppy slurp of his tongue. "Ooh boy, did I get slobbered that time!" I grinned and wiped my hand on the side of my skirt while the kids guffawed at the grossness of it all.

"But seriously, this is how Slugger learned to do so much. His trainer used positive rewards. Every time the dog did something right, she praised him and gave him a treat. Now that Slugger and I are a team, I always carry cheese with me. It's like an edible thank you to him."

I smiled and took a deep breath before continuing, "Believe it or not, service dogs can learn as many as fifty words. For example, Slugger knows the names of different things I use every day. We'll show you." Unzipping my dog's packs, I extracted a hairbrush, an empty pill bottle, and an old TV remote I kept for demonstrations. I held each item up before putting it on the floor. My Labrador's tail swished. Though he didn't know which object I'd request first, he loved showing off this skill. "Slugger," I said and then paused, building the suspense for my audience as well as for my dog, "pills!" He surveyed the items quickly, then fit his jaws around the bottle and placed it in my hand.

"Good dog!" I exclaimed while the children cheered. Next he retrieved the brush, and finally I asked for the remote. "Slugger seems to like bringing me this most of all!" I said, as I took the black rectangle from my dog. "I think that's because he always turns the channel to Animal Planet!"

The youngsters guffawed and I took the opportunity to reward my dog and get my hand-held phone out of Slugger's pack. This had a plastic handle attached to its side so it was easy for my dog to carry. Giving him the order to stay, I placed it on a table at the far end of the stage. As the laughter in the room quieted, I said, "Slugger will also get my phone for me. You'll see that in a minute." Then I returned to my seat. My dog draped his head atop my left foot. His spontaneous and affectionate move garnered an, "awwww!" from everyone in the room.

"How cute!" someone cooed.

To me, it was far more. Slugger's simple gesture affirmed our steadfast bond. He had believed in me before I knew how to believe in myself; now his unconditional love inspired me to move beyond a past filled with physical and emotional struggle. It wasn't easy to convey the depth of our bond, but I tried.

"Today we've been talking about how smart

Slugger is and how many words he knows. He also knows a lot about caring; he understands that truly caring for someone means sticking with that person. I can count on Slugger whenever and wherever I need him. As my specially trained partner, he goes with me to places where other dogs wouldn't set a paw. He works for me at home of course, and he helps me on the job, in the grocery store, in the doctor's office, in restaurants, and when we come out to meet folks like you too. He's even . . . "

Slugger suddenly lifted his head off my foot. He let out a loud, multi-syllable yawn. He was bored. I was upstaged. The kids were laughing their butts off. "I get the message," I chuckled, "too much talk, not enough action. Let's fix that."

The hysterics in the room gradually subsided, and I addressed my dog, "Get the phone!"

Slugger was across the stage in a flash. Reaching the table, he stood on his hind legs. His claws clicked against the tabletop as he placed his front paws there. He stretched forward and grasped the phone by its handle. Slugger didn't walk back to me then. No, my Labrador *pranced* across the stage. The phone dangling from his mouth bounced in perfect rhythm with his wagging tail.

"Lap," I said, raising my voice above the enthusiastic clapping of little hands. Obediently, Slugger placed the phone on my knees. "Thank you!" I took it, then gave him the *up* command. Now we were face to face. Warm and stinky puffs of dog breath greeted my nose, but I delighted in our closeness just the same. I bestowed a hug before telling the big Lab to get down.

Having asked one of the teachers to open the auditorium door nearest the stage, I prepared for our last task demonstration. Pointing, I said, "Finally folks, I'm going to send Slugger off the stage now and have him close that door over there."

"Won't he run away?" A youngster called out urgently.

"Oh no. Slugger is working right now, and he knows we are a team whether I am holding on to his leash or not." Now I asked my dog to stand. Bending forward so that my face was near his once more, I coaxed, "Okay, boy, are you ready?" The Lab's tail waved slowly. His bright eyes were focused and alert; they followed my hand as I gestured toward the open door. "Slugger, go close it!"

The big dog moved purposefully across the stage and down the steps. He trotted past the rows of fascinated children without so much as a distracted glance. He was on a mission!

When he reached the open door, Slugger positioned himself behind it and bumped it powerfully with his nose. The door slammed shut with an ear-splitting bang that echoed through the room. A few startled children squealed before joining their peers in giggles and applause. Clearly pleased with his own performance, Slugger turned and pranced back to me.

"Oh you are so good!" I took his leash and rewarded him with huge bite of cheese and an ear scratch.

Now I addressed the audience, "Our time is

almost up. We've covered a lot today, but there may be more you'd like to know. Any questions?"

Wiggly-fingered appendages sprouted instantly above the children's heads. "Yes?" I pointed to a curly-haired fellow with big blue eyes.

"How do you know when your dog has to pee?" He blurted out his question frantically, as if he'd wondered this for much of his young life. The other children giggled at his mention of a bodily function.

I'd learned long ago that this question was high on most people's list of *Top Ten Things You've Always Wanted to Know about Service Dogs.* I nodded. "An excellent question. It's important for Slugger to be comfortable and happy. I always take him outside for a bathroom break before we work together. If he needs to go while we are out somewhere, he lets me know by nudging my hand. Once I've found a patch of grass where he can take care of business, I tell him to *go park.*"

More questions followed. I found myself explaining that contrary to popular myth, my dog in fact liked cats, he never bit people (not even if they annoyed him), and he got to play and act like a regular dog when at home. A perceptive youngster asked, "Do people ever say mean things because you're different?"

This final question sparked a host of grim memories. But now, I reached down and stroked the top of Slugger's head. He looked into my eyes and waved his tail in sweet, unspoken affirmation.

"Sure," I answered. "I think that happens to everyone sometimes. But when it does, it helps to remember that differences are worth celebrating. It's important to believe in yourself and be your best you. In fact, that's what Slugger is all about; he helps me solve problems creatively so that I can be my very best!"

I rose slowly from my chair. Without prompting, Slugger moved into perfect heel position. "Thank you all very much for having us here today," I said. "Slugger and I really enjoyed our time with you!"

The school's principal joined us on stage. She smiled warmly, "Well, we sure have learned a lot from the two of you. Aren't they a great team, boys and girls?" she asked.

Hundreds of young voices boomed in unison, "Yeah!"

"What do we want to tell Ms. Brill and Slugger?"

Like a sudden summer storm, "Thank you!" thundered through the room and ushered in a torrent of frenzied clapping. I nodded and waved. As we made our way across the stage and down the steps, cheers began to punctuate the clapping. "Wahoo! Way to go! All right!"

A teacher approached us near the auditorium exit. "That," she said, gripping my hand in both of hers, "was just amazing!"

"Thanks, I'm glad you think so," I answered. "Of course it helps to have a top-notch partner." I looked down at my service dog and smiled.

Our admirer's gaze followed my own, and now she was smiling, too. "Slugger is really something, huh?"

"He is indeed," I said. "Something good."

Chapter 15

Decisions and Double Blessings

Retirement—just thinking about it put knots in my stomach. It wasn't my own retirement but Slugger's I dreaded. Our remarkable partnership had transformed my life; the idea of changing that partnership was so painful I scarcely allowed myself to consider it. Yet by the start of 2001, when Slugger was ten years old, I had no choice.

My hard-working Labrador had dealt with mild arthritis in his hips for a few years. Dr. Mark Finkler, our veterinarian and friend who also served on the Saint Francis board of directors, had prescribed supplements to help.

Happily, these pills did seem to lessen the stiffness in Slugger's back end. Since they also smelled like the marsh at low tide, I only had to call out, "Pill time!" and Slugger would be at my side in an instant. I doubt he realized the medicinal value of his daily tablets. To him they were simply glorious bites of stinkiness!

Eventually however, even those well-loved and

effective supplements couldn't stop the effects of time. An X-ray revealed that the arthritis in Slugger's hips had progressed from mild to moderate.

"It's certainly something that's treatable," Dr. Finkler said softly as the two of us stood in the exam room of Roanoke Animal Hospital. "And it's not a real big issue for a regular pet. But for a working dog...".

I looked at my big yellow dog, who stood on the shiny metal exam table, wagging and panting. Then I looked at the films of his hip bones. Even my untrained eyes could discern the arthritis there. "It's kind of strange," I said, feeling suddenly annoyed at the lump that rose in my throat. "When we work together, he seems just fine. I've noticed he gets tired some days and sometimes we both walk more slowly than we used to. But it's not like he ever stops walking or refuses to work. I mean he never acts like he's in pain."

"Yeah," Dr. Finkler's tone was gentle. He seemed to be speaking to me and to my dog at the same time. "Slugger wouldn't. When he's with you, he's focused on his job, not his pain. Unfortunately, that doesn't mean the pain's not there." The doctor scratched Slugger's chin affectionately.

"Right, I see your point," I said, recalling the time he had refused to break work mode even when I'd accidentally hurt him. I was crying freely now. I knew with every fiber of my being, I couldn't ask my beloved service dog to continue working for me if it caused him pain.

Years ago Slugger's trainer, Vickie, had passed

him on to me saying, "You'll both take care of each other. That's how it works." At the time I hadn't grasped the full scope of her words. Now I understood. "So I have to make this decision for Slugger, in his best interest, don't I?"

"I can't tell you what to do," Dr. Finkler answered, "but that's what I'd do if he were my own dog. He can still help with lighter tasks around the house of course, and he should be fine with occasional outings. But I'd say it's time for Slugger to start enjoying his well-earned retirement."

As I left the clinic, I couldn't argue with the X-ray evidence or Dr. Finkler's kindly guidance. Slugger was ready for his retirement. My heart was another matter.

Loading Slugger into the back of the car, I wiped my face with a Kleenex and slid into the driver's seat. The trip home felt much longer than the actual miles that stretched between the vet's office and our house; waves of sadness washed over me as I drove.

"Oh, sweet dog," I said, peering in the rearview mirror at him. He sensed my heightened emotion. He sat up and stared back at me with raised ears and an intense expression that seemed to ask, *What's wrong?*

I halted my car at a red light. A van had pulled up alongside; its young passenger gawked at me from behind smudged windows. I grabbed my crumpled Kleenex and dabbed my eyes, but somehow the motion only brought on fresh tears.

"Things have to be different now, Sluggie, and I need you to know it's for your own good," I said as the light turned and the traffic crept forward. "I won't be asking you to work so much. We won't be going out as often either. God, I wish things could be the way they've always been, but I can't stand the thought of you helping me while you're in pain. I love you too much to allow that. You understand, don't you?" This was all I knew to say, all I had the strength to say. I listened to Slugger's soft panting then, and I sobbed.

That evening I discussed the results of Slugger's visit to the vet with Pranav. "Time for his gold watch," I said, trying to lighten the news as much for myself as for Pranav. "Or maybe I ought to say it's time for his gold collar."

"Well, if any dog deserves a gold collar, it's Sluggie."

Hearing raw emotion in my husband's voice, I felt tears rise yet again in my eyes. Pranav passed me a tissue, and for a while neither of us said anything.

Eventually Slugger seemed to think it was time to liven things up. He grabbed one of his favorite stuffed toys, a ratty little Winnie the Pooh. Then he trotted over to Pranav and plonked it in his lap.

The gesture made us laugh. It also confirmed that while significant adjustments lay ahead, some things wouldn't change. For Slugger, today had simply been another day of hanging out with me, making the most of every moment. And he clearly thought *this* moment was perfect for playing.

Pranav picked up the smelly little toy and began

making it dance through the air. Mesmerized by his jigging bear, Slugger lowered his front end in a play bow. He let out a long, musical howl, *Ooooowowwow!*

"It sounds like somebody has some pretty good ideas about how he'd like to fill his retirement!" Pranav said.

Indeed, in the weeks that followed, Slugger often came up to Pranav and me and offered a toy for a quick game of fetch or tug. He seemed happy with the relaxed pace of his retirement, though he still took it upon himself to pick up things I dropped around the house.

He also relished helping with laundry; I'd attached a pulling strap to my laundry basket and my Lab had always loved towing it to and from the washer for me. Now, to make that job easier, I filled the basket only half way. Slugger was delighted to prance around the house on washday, tugging his lighter loads to their destinations.

Shortly before his retirement, I'd decided to make some changes to my own life. Aware that the physical challenges of my disability were increasing, I got a wheelchair to use on more demanding days; and although I loved working with the staff, volunteers, and guests at Ronald McDonald House, I decided to focus on my writing full time.

Fortunately, that meant I didn't have to head off to work and leave Slugger at home every day. He'd curl up under my computer desk as I wrote, providing instant inspiration for my dog-themed stories and occasional, much needed work breaks.

Spending time with Slugger gave me a comforting

sense that our partnership, though different now, remained strong. I always let him come along for quick errands, and I found myself avoiding the longer outings that would be too much for him all together. When such solo trips were absolutely necessary, I tried to make our partings as easy on Slugger as possible. I'd invite him onto the couch and cuddle with him before leaving.

Pranav had wisely suggested keeping some dog treats on the table by our front door, and I'd grab a large Milk-bone from that stash whenever I had to go out without Slugger. Offering it to him, I'd promise, "Be right back, sweet dog. See you soon."

This exit ritual helped ease my guilt at leaving my partner behind. Happily, it seemed to satisfy Slugger as well; though I expected he might respond to our separation by diving into the nearest trash can, the Labrador rarely resorted to those antics now.

Instead he chose to take advantage of a quiet house by stretching out for a nap right in the middle of my bed.

I was pleased that Slugger was willing to take things easy. Yet for me, going out alone was frustrating and difficult. I often used a wooden cane to steady myself while walking, but this was more cumbersome and less effective than the canine assistant I'd grown to trust.

Alone I tripped often, I bumped into things and people, and I grew more and more exhausted. Although my wheelchair helped on days when my legs were especially wobbly, I still felt lonely whenever Slugger was not at my side.

I'd move through a busy grocery store, trying to concentrate on my shopping list. But if I allowed my awareness to go deeper than *onions, paper towels, hand lotion, and seafood if it's on sale*, I encountered an aching emptiness, as if I were trying to function without a part of myself.

Months passed, and though Slugger had adapted more smoothly than I'd anticipated to his new slower life, I still missed the physical security and the constant companionship I'd had with my working canine. I knew it was possible to bring a young service dog into a home with a retired one; many people, including my friend Carol, chose to do that. Cautiously, slowly, I rolled the idea around in my mind: *Should I get a second dog?*

At first even asking the question filled me with guilt. I worried that forming a new working partnership with a young dog would be a betrayal of my bond with Slugger. Yet I also knew I needed the benefits that only service dog partnership could provide.

Unsure what to do, I confided in those closest to me—Pranav and Carol. Pranav sensed the heaviness of my dilemma. He listened with an open heart and didn't push me one way or the other. I was grateful for his understanding when he promised, "Two dogs might be a handful, but if that's what you need, we'll find a way to make it work. I'll support the choice you feel is best."

Then, in true littermate fashion, Carol helped me make that choice. Feeling torn apart by uncertainty, I phoned her one afternoon and tearfully confessed my inner conflict of guilt and need. In a quiet, soothing voice she said, "Leigh, do you think Slugger knows you love him as much as he loves you?"

"Yes," I answered.

"And given that, don't you think he wants what's best for you?"

"Absolutely."

Carol spoke slowly as she posed a final question, "Did you ever stop to think Slugger might actually *enjoy* having another dog be a part of his life, too?"

"Oh my God," I said. Suddenly I realized I'd been looking at this issue from a negative point of view, as if bringing a second dog into my home would somehow replace Slugger.

But Carol's words gave me permission to see it differently. I smiled. "You know, you're right! Maybe Sluggie *would* like that. After all, he had played an important role when I formed a family with Pranav. If any dog could oversee the addition of a new family member now, it's him!"

"I bet he'd be a great teacher for a young dog too. Professor Slugger!" Carol laughed.

By the time I'd thanked her and hung up the phone, I was laughing too.

I thought about Carol's words for weeks. And the more I thought about them the more convinced I became. I wanted my beloved Labrador and my second dog—whoever that turned out to be— to know each other, to be a part of each other's lives. No doubt the youngster would learn a lot from Slugger. And now I had a hunch that dog would brighten Slugger's days as well.

By summer, my family of three was ready to expand—we were officially prepared to add one more tail-wagging member. Unfortunately I'd received the news that Caring Canine Companions had disbanded. Remembering my life-changing experiences with Vickie and Sylvia, I felt pangs of regret and sadness.

I knew, however, that the trainers with Saint Francis Service Dogs might be able to help me. Since becoming involved with the foundation, I'd met many of the dogs in their program.

These animals were beautiful, well mannered, and highly skilled. Knowing it would be an honor to be partnered with one of them, I spoke with several trainers and submitted an application to become a candidate for my second service dog.

I felt nervous on the afternoon Karen Hough, the training director, came to my home for my required screening interview. As a member of the foundation's screening committee myself, I knew basically what to expect from our visit.

We reviewed my specific physical issues and needs, discussed my lifestyle, and talked about the type of dog I'd feel most comfortable with. Still, I worried that it'd be especially difficult to find a dog that could work well with me *and* share our home with a retired service dog.

"It sounds a little backwards," I said sheepishly, as Karen and I sat chatting in my living room, "but if a match is going to work for me, it has to work for Slugger first. At some level I guess I want his okay with all this, you know?"

"Of course," Karen said kindly. "He deserves

that. Any match we make will have to be a good fit for everyone—humans and canines!"

Karen's understanding eased my anxieties, and I appreciated her promise at the end of our visit as well. "Because you've been partnered with Slugger for so many years and now need a second service dog to take over his work duties," she said, "I'll do my best to find the perfect one for you as soon as possible."

"Thank you, Karen, that sounds great," I answered. But as I walked her to the door, the voice inside my head said, *Even with her efforts, you'd best be prepared for quite a wait; service dogs—especially perfect ones—don't grow on trees.*

It wasn't long before I discovered that even if they didn't grow on trees, perfect service dogs could look mighty cute sitting under them. True to her word, Karen had moved quickly in her quest for my second dog.

Only a few short months after our meeting, I found myself gazing at one of the dearest pups I'd ever seen. Dr. Finkler and his wife, Beth, had donated the two-year-old female yellow Lab named Kenda to Saint Francis Service Dogs.

Now she was seated next to her trainer, Mitzi Tinaglia. The pair waited in the shade of a towering tree as I hurried across my yard toward them.

"Hey there!" Mitzi's cheerful greeting was familiar; we'd spoken by phone several times before deciding to get together so that Slugger and Kenda could meet each other.

I wanted to begin by spending a few minutes focused on the young dog and her trainer; for now,

Slugger had to wait in the house. I felt sure he'd take an instant shine to Mitzi thanks to her bubbly personality and endless supply of dog treats. But how would he feel about Kenda?

Had I summed up my first impression of her using a human reference, I would've said Kenda resembled Audrey Hepburn. But I figured that description might sound odd to someone I'd only recently met, so I settled for, "Oh my gosh, Mitzi, she's adorable!"

When I reached down to pet the dog, she wagged her tail and twitched her diminutive nose. Her long whiskers tickled against my skin as she sniffed lightly up and down my arm. I noticed those whiskers were curled on the ends, making it look as if they'd been styled to achieve maximum cuteness.

Her sparkly eyes were framed by perfect dark outlines. I grinned at Mitzi. "Looks like you gussied her up with eyeliner for our meeting!"

"Kenda's just a natural beauty! Can you imagine looking *that* good without having to get out the trusty old Cover Girl?" The dog's trainer laughed.

But of course, when I brought Slugger outside a few minutes later, he didn't give a hoot about Kenda's lovely eyes, or her curly whiskers, or any other aspect of her appearance. He was all dog—his only interest was her smell.

Mitzi had slipped Kenda's working packs off, and my dog stuck his nose in the new dog's butt. Before long the two yellow Labs engaged in a sniffing, prancing, circling routine that Mitzi and I agreed ought to be set to music.

Happily, neither dog seemed upset. They frolicked and bounced around each other. Caught up in the excitement, Kenda let out a hearty *woof, woof, woof, woof!* That's when I discovered that the little dog's voice didn't exactly match her appearance. Sure, she looked like Audrey Hepburn, but her rich, jazzy voice was closer to the canine equivalent of Ella Fitzgerald's!

When Slugger had finished giving this vocal girl the once, twice, and thrice over, he begged a treat from Mitzi and then stretched out at my feet. Kenda settled beside her trainer. Her ears, which unlike her other parts, were bigger than Slugger's, raised, and she looked around. The inquisitive expression on her face seemed to ask, *Now what?*

After the success of the dogs' introductions, Mitzi and I took them both inside and chatted for a while. Slugger lay down on the fluffy plaid cushion Pranav and I referred to as his "daybed;" from this vantage point he could easily watch the goings on in the living room, the kitchen, and the front entrance.

Now he cradled his pooh bear between his front paws, shifting his gaze from me, to Kenda, to Mitzi, then back to me. Mitzi had grabbed one of Kenda's toys out of her car, and the Lab sat gnawing on it with a gusto that reminded me of a lioness over her kill.

"Good gracious!" I said, "She's really going after that . . . ah, what *is* that?"

"Oh, she's got one of those nylon dog Frisbees. Loves those things!" Mitzi reached down and stroked Kenda's ear lovingly. "She destroyed two before this!" As if to prove the point, Kenda grabbed one edge of her toy and yanked it. There was a loud ripping sound.

Mitzi rolled her eyes, "I've tried to teach her, *no tear,* but sometimes she gets carried away." She reached down and said, "Kenda, give." Instantly the little Lab relinquished her toy, which now hung in strips. "Don't think this one's going to last much longer!" Mitzi tucked the stringy thing in her purse, leaving Kenda to stare wistfully up at her.

Eventually the toyless pup became bored. She got up, sniffed around the living room and wandered into the kitchen. I smiled to see this svelte little creature investigating the house. Though she was the same breed as Slugger, she looked quite different from my sturdy, barrel-chested dog.

Where Slugger's coat was thick and fluffy, Kenda's was sleek and slightly coarse. Her tail sat higher than Slugger's and her head was proportionately smaller than his. Though I was quick to avow Slugger's classic good looks, I had to admit this new little Labrador was a charmer.

I'd been worried I might subconsciously expect a second working partner to be just like Slugger, but after spending a short time with Kenda, I knew that wouldn't be a problem. Kenda was her own dog!

Unfortunately, she was now her own dog *without* her own toy. After trotting past Slugger several times, bouncing up and down in front of him, and eyeing him coyly, Kenda plucked up her nerve. Tail wagging, she pranced right up to her elder and nosed her way toward his prized pooh bear.

Slugger let out a low, no-nonsense growl.

Kenda cocked her head but didn't move away.

If his first growl had been the canine version of

Don't even think about it, whippersnapper, then Slugger's second snarl was clearly, *I said no!*

Fearing a tussle was in the works, I shot Mitzi a wide-eyed look. "They're okay," she said quietly. "It's important to let the dogs sort things out on their own terms."

Thankfully, this time Kenda seemed to agree to those terms. She backed up, then turned and walked purposefully into the kitchen as if recalling something there she just had to check out right this minute.

"Did Slugger teach you a quick lesson in boundaries, girlie?" I gave her a quick pat when she returned to the living room. The little Lab's tongue flicked across my hand.

Not surprisingly, that wasn't Kenda's only lesson courtesy of Slugger. She and Mitzi made regular visits to our home following that first meeting. And though Slugger sometimes had to relax with a good bone in the back bedroom while I worked with Kenda and her trainer, he lived up to the title Carol had bestowed.

Professor Slugger offered some paws-on assistance one day when Mitzi was helping me practice retrieves with Kenda. Like Slugger, Kenda had been trained to get her leash on command. But on this particular day, the sharp young pup was bouncier, less focused, than usual.

I'd put Slugger on a *down-stay* on his daybed and I knew his presence could be the cause of her distraction. Still, I hoped that carefully including him at times like this would help both dogs adjust to their new roles and to each other.

Kenda had completed two successful retrieves—

getting her leash off the floor and placing it in my hands—when Mitzi said, "Let's change it up!" Now she placed the leather lead on a nearby coffee table.

I gave the command, "Kenda, leash!" The little Lab looked at me. She looked at the floor. She looked at me again. Then she swung her head from side to side. Having lost both her leash and her focus, she began hopping straight up and down in a manner that would eventually inspire me to give her the nickname Meerkat.

As if unimpressed by his successor's antics, Slugger slowly got up from his bed. He ambled over to the coffee table and scooped Kenda's leash into his mouth. Mitzi and I watched in amazed silence as he walked up to Kenda and dropped the leash in front of her bouncing body.

The little dog picked it up then. She tossed her head proudly before depositing her recovered lead into my hand.

"That's what I call some serious teamwork!" I bent down and hugged first Slugger and then his wiggling protégé.

When my own teamwork with Kenda began to strengthen, the two of us took part in the foundation's weekly group training classes. Then we started working together in public, meeting Mitzi at the mall and in restaurants.

Although Slugger couldn't join us for these outings, I still felt his presence; long before he'd helped Kenda with her leash retrieval, he had taught me the essentials of service dog partnership. The triumphs and mistakes I'd shared with him served as valuable lessons as I forged a new working relationship with my second canine partner.

With these lessons in mind I was able to relax and enjoy the process of getting to know Kenda. I quickly discovered that she was a thinker—I could almost see her brain go into problem-solving mode when I'd ask her to punch an elevator button with her nose or carry my prescriptions from the pharmacy.

In no time she began to offer me these and other helpful behaviors before I'd even asked for them! Kenda was also very sensitive, much more so than her predecessor.

While that meant she was cooperative and easy to work with, it also meant I had to keep my interactions with her low-key when she was on the job. Thankfully, like Slugger, my second service dog was intelligent and hardworking; so with Mitzi's expert guidance, Kenda and I eventually found our own working rhythm. It was both smooth and unique, a sweet variation of the cadence I'd first known with Slugger.

Kenda and I graduated in November of that year, and though our official training was successfully completed now, our at-home lessons with Professor Slugger were destined to continue. At least a little while longer.

Early one morning during the first week of Kenda's arrival, I awoke to the sight of big, brown, twitching nostrils. They were familiar; Slugger's head was resting on the edge of the bed as usual, and this morning he seemed to think that positioning his snout a mere whisker's width away from my face would earn him a speedy ear scratch.

He was right. Half awake, I mumbled, "Hey, bud." I stuck out my fingers and started massaging. Just when my yellow fellow was about to go into a trance, I noticed a flutter of movement.

Standing directly behind Slugger, with her ears perked and her tail wagging, was Kenda. In my groggy, bleary-eyed state, I'd not realized she was there. "Well, good morning to you too, girlie," I said. "Looks like the gang's all here."

I might as well have shouted, "Ready, set, go!" Slugger suddenly backed up, grabbed a sock off the floor and bolted out of the room.

I laughed at his sock-napping routine, but poor Kenda, who'd had to jump out of the way as Slugger dashed past her, looked dazed. She glanced at me, tossed her head, then trotted out of the room after Slugger.

I'd come to realize that my lovely little girl dog had an overachiever, straight-A streak not unlike my own, and it was clear she didn't want to miss any of Professor Slugger's morning class.

I was fairly certain Kenda earned high marks in that class because the next day's sock-napping had a twist. No sooner had Slugger grabbed a bedside sock then his understudy swooped in and nabbed the sneaker that had been sitting next to it!

The two Labs took off through the house. I stayed still a few moments and listened to the bittersweet sound—the now slow thud of Slugger's gallop, joined by the scuttling of eager young paws.

Slugger's s hesitant gait made it clear his arthritis

was worsening, and by his eleventh year, his eyesight began to dim as well. Dr. Finkler assured me these changes were due to the natural aging process. Still, Slugger's steadfast strength had been my foundation for so many years; I ached to see this decline.

When I took my two dogs out for a game of fetch, I would fling Kenda's toy far out across the yard. But I now tossed Slugger's more lightly, making a point to aim it toward the flattest part of the lawn. True to his retriever heritage, my boy still relished every game of fetch he could get.

He'd scamper after his beloved Pooh bear and return panting, with a look that said, *One more?* But since becoming a multidog family, I'd taught my Labs to take turns. Pooh wouldn't take flight again until after I'd launched Kenda's favorite stuffed duck.

This orderly approach to the game avoided both confusion and potential scuffles. Fortunately, both dogs were willing to follow the rules—it wasn't long before all I had to say was, "This one's Slugger's," or, "This is for Kenda." The other Lab would then move out of the way and wait for the next throw.

One day while engaged in our organized game, I accidentally tossed Slugger's toy further into the yard than usual. My older dog trotted in the direction of the throw and stopped short. He couldn't see his little stuffed bear perched in the grass several feet away. Feeling bad to have confused him, I called, "It's okay, boy. I'll come help!"

But before I'd started across the yard, Kenda began hopping up and down beside me. I reached down and rubbed her ear. "What is it, Meerkat? I'll be right back, I just have to go get—" I stopped then and looked at my bouncing dog.

She'd not gone after Slugger's favorite stuffed bear even once since he had snarled at her on her very first visit. *Surely she's not planning to steal the bear now,* I thought. *She probably just has to pee.*

Almost as soon as I said, "Okay, Kenda, go on!" I regretted it. She ran straight for Slugger's toy. *Crap,* the voice in my head fussed, *you should've known better than to do that!* The speedy little dog reached Slugger's bear in a flash.

I expected her to grab it and make a mad dash around the yard. She didn't. With her ears perked and her tail wagging, Kenda turned to face Slugger. She just stood there looking at him. She didn't make the slightest move to get his toy. Amazed, I realized: *She's actually showing Slugger where it is!*

He walked over to Kenda, looked down, and then picked up his bear. Tears filled my eyes as I watched the two dogs walk back toward me. Kenda, it seemed, was happy to be a service dog's service dog when the need arose!

After that day, I noticed she kept a close eye on Slugger whenever we went outside. Any time he was unable to locate his toy, she would repeat her helpful maneuver. And when the older dog would stretch out for a nap—as he did frequently these days—Kenda made a habit of trotting up to him and bestowing a single gentle lick on the top of his head. He'd wag once or twice in response, sigh, and then drift back to sleep.

It always touched my heart to see this. Kenda

seemed to understand that at some level Slugger and I each needed her help. And in her sweet, lively way, she let us both know, *Don't worry, I've got your back!* Years had passed since Slugger's trainer first reminded me that a service dog is a dog; yet now as I shared my life and my heart with two incredible Labs, it was sometimes easy to forget the implications of that truth. I'd look at Slugger and Kenda lying in the grass on a sunny afternoon and simply marvel at my double blessings.

But soon I'd have to face the truth. A service dog is a dog. And dogs—even the best ones—cannot live forever.

Chapter 16

A Promise Returned

Bright lights blinked from the eaves of buildings and winked from the branches of trees. Wreaths festooned doors, and a feeling of celebration hung in the air as sweet and heady as the smell of baking gingerbread. Although I tried to get into the spirit of the Christmas holiday in 2002, I couldn't. I was too worried about Slugger.

His occasional bouts of vomiting that had started a few weeks ago were now more persistent. At first I'd switched his dog food to a diet of rice and tried to dismiss the problem, reminding myself that all dogs get sick sometimes.

Besides, the voice in my head had said, *no need to over-worry things; it's probably just a passing tummy ache. He's had those before.*

Slugger acted like his normal happy self and he finished off every meal with his usual gusto; so for a while I could make myself believe my rationalizations. But whatever had a hold on him had ramped up markedly now.

Suddenly my poor dog couldn't make it more than two days in a row without heaving up the contents of his stomach. I cringed every time I heard the horrid gracking that sounded as if Slugger were trying to rid himself of all his internal organs.

I made an appointment for him to see Dr. Finkler as soon as his office opened after the holidays. In the meantime I moved Slugger's bed into the living room and built a nest for myself on the couch.

That way I could at least keep a close eye on Slugger overnight and let him out when he needed it. Some nights he would wake me, prancing anxiously and smacking his lips. I'd race from my makeshift bed and fling the front door open so that he could go out into the yard to vomit.

The frigid night air whipped around me then as if it longed to join the icy fear growing within my heart. I stood in the doorway waiting for my sick Lab, and I prayed, *Whatever this is, please God, let it be fixable.*

When Slugger returned, he always seemed in a hurry to get back to sleep. He'd trot indoors with his tail waving, and go straight to his bed as if to say, *Now that that's taken care of, maybe we can get some shut-eye.*

The eventual sound of his snores told me he was resting peacefully. But for me, sleep was out of the question. I'd huddle on the couch for hours watching my beloved dog, wondering, and trying not to cry.

I was still trying to hold back tears on the afternoon Pranav and I took Slugger to see Dr. Finkler. He'd slotted us into the first available appointment in the new year, and as he carefully examined my dog now, our friend's concern was obvious.

"Slugger's peripheral lymph nodes—those near the surface of the skin—are enlarged. That's not something we like to see," Dr. Finkler said gently. He stroked Slugger's head and continued. "It's often an indication of lymphoma. I'd like to do a blood panel and urinalysis in order to get a clearer picture of things. I think we should also schedule a biopsy of a lymph node to confirm the diagnosis."

Though I'd been coaching myself to stay calm, I felt suddenly dizzy, unable to breathe. Standing beside the metal exam table, I clamped my sweaty fingers around its edge in a desperate attempt to steady myself. I swallowed hard and fought to speak coherently. My lips, like my mind, had begun to go numb. "You mean you think he might have cancer?" I whispered.

"Well, I don't know for sure. But it's pretty common in dogs Slugger's age, and given his swollen lymph nodes, there's a possibility that's what we're dealing with. So I'd like to get him in for a biopsy as soon as possible if that's okay with you."

"Okay, yes, as soon as possible," I stammered.

"I know this is a lot to take in all at once," Dr. Finkler said kindly. "Can you have Slugger here tomorrow morning between seven and seven-thirty? Then you can pick him up at the end of the day."

Now Pranav, who'd been silent for most of the visit, said, "Of course! We'll have him here." His proclamation came out hoarse, adamant, and strained with emotion.

After sorting out the details for the dog's surgery, we paid our bill at the front desk. Now my heart, my emotions were completely numb. My brain had shifted into its protective mode, only venturing basic directives: *Take Slugger out the front door. Load him into the car. Get into the passenger's seat. Hold onto the papers we'll need for tomorrow's appointment. Sit still. Look out the window. Don't feel.*

It seemed my husband was in shock too. He stayed home from work for the rest of that day. We barely spoke, not even to our beloved Slugger or bouncy, sweet little Kenda. I knew Pranav and I should discuss things, voice some sort of solace for one another. But for now I wrapped myself in the insulation of silence.

It wasn't until night came, with its own unavoidable stillness, that feeling came back to me. Sensation returned like the sting of frozen fingers thawed by a fire in winter, but it was a million times sharper in my heart. I didn't sleep—I didn't even try. Instead I settled on the floor next to Slugger's bed.

He was curled there. He eyed me and licked his jowls several times as if trying to figure out exactly why he'd had to go without his supper this evening and why I was now sitting so close to him with my hand resting motionless on his head. I sat that way for a long time, not daring to move.

My partnership with Slugger had long been bound by his unspoken and unchanging promise. Now I could only return that promise; gazing into his beautiful face, I whispered, "Whatever happens, I'm here for you. I'm here for you no matter what."

Slugger sighed and shifted on his bed.

He rested his head in my lap. Tears ran like rivers from my eyes then. They soaked into his thick fur as I talked to him. "Tomorrow's going to be rough; you'll go through pain. I'm sorry, I wish it didn't have to be that way. But you need more help that I can give; you have to have this surgery. Dr. Finkler will take good care of you. And we'll get through this the best we can. Together."

As if tuned in to the importance and pain of this moment, Kenda got up from her own bed. She walked softly over to me, forgoing her usual bounce. Then she stretched out at my side and draped one leg across my thigh so that her paw rested near Slugger's. Surprised and comforted, I whispered, "Hey, girlie." After that, the long dark hours were soundless except for my dogs' nocturnal murmurings, my muted sobs, and the ticking of the clock.

I'd lost all sense of time when Pranav eventually trudged out of the bedroom. He was bleary-eyed and dazed. "Did you stay out here all night?"

I rubbed a hand across my swollen face. "Yeah, what's the time?"

"Five-thirty. Figured I should get up early so I could get ready for work and have plenty of time to get Slugger over to Dr. Finkler as soon as the hospital opens."

"Right," I mumbled as Pranav rubbed my shoulders and planted a kiss on top of my head. He bestowed good morning ear scratches to both dogs and shuffled into the kitchen to put the coffee on. When he returned a few minutes later to offer me a hot mug, I refused.

"Thanks anyway. I'll get some later." Stress and exhaustion were exacting their physical toll and now the usually pleasant smell of coffee made my stomach lurch. I suddenly felt so light-headed and queasy that I barely made it to the bathroom before throwing up.

Though I'd planned on accompanying Pranav to take Slugger to Dr. Finkler's office, I quickly decided that was a bad idea. If I couldn't trust myself not to throw up or pass out, I'd be no help to my husband or my sick dog.

Plus, I knew if I went along, Slugger would be upset by my current state. I didn't want him worried about me as he went into surgery. So I hugged and kissed my beloved Labrador and watched from the front porch later that morning as Pranav loaded him into our Honda and drove to the animal hospital.

Only when the car had completely vanished from my sight did I venture back into the house. I closed the door softly and leaned against its coldness. Slowly I crumpled onto the floor. Anguish washed over me then and I howled.

Kenda stood nearby, watching me with a quizzical expression. She seemed uncomfortable, unsure what to do. But just as I had begun to feel guilty about distressing her, the little dog came toward me. Lightly she licked my hand over and over as if she were trying to soothe my pain. I pulled her to me and hugged her until I had the strength to stand up.

Kenda's sweet presence calmed me. I fixed her breakfast, took her outside, and gave her thick winter coat a thorough brushing. These familiar routines brought a little bit of normalcy and purpose to the morning hours. They comforted me too. Until the phone rang.

I was simultaneously relieved and nervous to hear Dr. Finkler's voice when he called to give me an update at noon. "Slugger made it through the surgery fine," he assured me.

I'd been holding my breath without realizing it; I exhaled loudly now, "Great! That's good news!"

Dr. Finkler's words were measured and sensitive when he added, "You'll need to bring Slugger back in a few days. We'll have his biopsy results by then, and we can determine the best course of action going forward. In the meantime he should be ready to go home by this evening. For now, just try and keep him as comfortable as possible while he recuperates."

Keeping Slugger comfortable was harder than I'd imagined. When Pranav brought him home from the hospital that evening, Slugger was restless and still groggy from his ordeal. It wasn't until we grabbed one of the big fluffy throw pillows off the couch and tucked it beneath Slugger's shoulders and head that he was finally able to settle down.

As had become my habit, I slept on the couch again that night to keep an eye on him. Though I felt stiff and bedraggled by morning, I knew my discomfort was nothing compared to Slugger's. From that time on, my existence took on a singular focus. I only wanted to be there for the dog who had always been there for me.

Our return visit to the animal hospital a few days later was a family affair. I wanted—I needed—my spouse and both dogs around me then. Dr. Finkler offered the same combination of professionalism and sensitivity I'd come to appreciate so much over the past few weeks. His voice was soft when he said, "Unfortunately the results of the biopsy confirm what we were afraid of—Slugger has lymphoma."

Shock moved through me then, numbing like anesthetic while Dr. Finkler explained Slugger's condition. Lymphoma, he said, is a fast-growing malignancy.

It can show up anywhere there is lymph tissue, which includes virtually every organ in the body. Eventually, the cancer will infiltrate an organ so completely that the organ fails; very often this is the bone marrow or the liver. I blanched when the veterinarian went on to say that the average life expectancy for a patient with untreated lymphoma is about two months from the time of diagnosis.

"What," my voice cracked. "What can we do?"

"Well the good news is if we start Slugger on a course of chemotherapy, there's a strong chance we can achieve remission," Dr. Finkler answered. "There's no telling if that will happen for sure or how long it may last, but it's a chance to give him a little more time. Fortunately, most dogs don't experience complications from chemotherapy.

While Slugger may lose his whiskers, he won't

lose all his fur, and he's not likely to have any other negative side effects."

This small bit of positive news gave me the courage to voice the truth in my heart. Yet it was so difficult I felt as if I were somehow above the scene, watching and listening to my own painful, disjointed declaration. "The main thing here, I want to do whatever we can. Of course, we have to do that. It's just that, the main thing, I don't want him to suffer for my sake." I gasped, "Even if it means our time together is less, I can't ask him for that, not after all he's given me."

I suddenly felt completely drained, as if the words that passed through my lips had taken every bit of my strength with them. Sobbing, I blinked at Dr. Finkler and added meekly, "You know?"

His reply was gentle. "We can fight the cancer and do everything possible to maintain a decent quality of life for Slugger at the same time."

"Yes," I said. "He deserves that. And if—when—that's no longer possible, promise you'll tell me? So I can do right by him?"

"I promise."

With Dr. Finkler's guidance we decided on a treatment protocol that would involve weekly chemo for Slugger. Then we invested a small fortune in canned dog food specifically formulated for animals fighting cancer. Dr. Finkler warned us that many dogs didn't like the taste of this food, that it'd be wise to add some cooked beef or chicken into Slugger's meals.

So we stopped by the grocery store on the way

home from the hospital and stocked up on as much meat as we could fit into our freezer.

Cooking hamburger and chicken, mixing it in with Slugger's new canned food, gave me a small sense of control in the days that followed—this was one practical thing I could do to help him fight his cancer. And the enthusiasm with which Slugger approached each meal now warmed my heart. He seemed, if anything, more ravenous for his new diet than I'd ever seen him. I took this as a good sign. He was getting the specialized nutrition he needed. And he was enjoying it!

Thanks to this diet and the chemotherapy, Slugger's health improved over the next few weeks. Gradually his lymph nodes began to reduce in size, and his horrible bouts of vomiting ceased. For a time the good days outnumbered the bad. "He didn't throw up even once today!" I'd report cheerily into the phone when my husband called over his lunch hour. Then I'd tell Slugger, "Pranav phoned to check up on you."

I told my beloved Labrador many things that winter. I reminisced about the times we'd shared. I rambled on about everyday things like silly television shows and the weather, and of course I talked about his little protégé, Kenda.

Most of all, I told Slugger how good he was, how much I loved him. I spent hours just sitting and stroking the dog's soft fur. The ear scratches once relegated to our morning routine were now bestowed every few hours, and on especially good days, when Slugger seemed to feel up to it, we'd go outside with

Kenda prancing happily along, and enjoy a fun—if abbreviated—game of fetch.

Still, our happiness was overshadowed by an inescapable truth. Dr. Finkler had told us that the chemo would certainly prolong Slugger's life. But it wouldn't cure him. Eventually the lymphoma would become resistant to therapy.

I scarcely allowed myself to think about that time. I wanted to believe that these sweet and quiet days with Slugger could go on and on. He could rest, eat chicken and hamburger, and play a bit when he got the urge. And he could stay with me.

But late one Sunday night in early March, I awoke to a familiar gut-wrenching sound. Slugger was throwing up more violently than he'd ever done before.

"Oh sweet dog!" I cried, rushing to his side. A true gentleman even in his darkest moments, Slugger staggered toward the door to be let out. He seemed bothered to have made a mess in the house; as soon as I opened the door he somehow managed to get his retching self into the yard. When he came back inside a few minutes later, his step was slow. His tail was completely still.

"Sluggie?" I whispered, knowing my sensitive dog would hear the fear in my voice, "Sluggie?"

He lifted his head then and met my gaze. But my beloved Lab's eyes looked strange to me; their familiar spark was gone. Now they seemed dull and distant, empty of all but one thing—pain.

I stayed awake with Slugger the rest of that night. Through my tears I watched him pace round and round the living room. Though I tried to console my dog, petting him, talking to him, even offering him a bite of chicken, my efforts made little difference.

He was too restless, too uncomfortable to focus on me. My heart sank when my normally food-crazed Lab even refused his chicken snack. So I watched him pace, and I did the only thing I could. *Please God,* I prayed, *don't let this be the end, not here, not now when I can't even ease his pain.*

We rushed Slugger to the animal hospital first thing the next morning. Though Dr. Finkler wasn't in the office that day, I was grateful when his colleague Dr. Bridget Quatmann met us at the door.

She'd nursed Slugger through a paw injury a few years ago, and she and my lady-charmer Lab had formed a fast bond. Now the doctor looked him over. She gazed into his eyes. "He's not his usual self," I said, noting the worried expression that clouded the doctor's pretty face.

"No, he's not, is he?" she said softly. "Think we need to take this boy back and get him on pain medication right away. Once he's comfortable, we'll do some tests and find out exactly what's going on. Okay?" She patted Slugger's side gently and for a moment I wasn't sure if her question was for me or for him.

I bit my lip and nodded. Then I bent down and kissed the top of Slugger's head. "It's gonna be okay now, sweet boy. They'll take care of you and give you something for the pain. It's gonna be okay now." I couldn't bring myself to say good-bye, so I simply kissed him once more and turned to leave.

As she walked Slugger slowly through the side door leading to the treatment area, Dr. Quatmann called, "I'll phone you just as soon as we know something."

It was afternoon when her call came. And the news she had to share was what I'd been expecting and dreading since the night before. Tearfully, Dr. Quatmann told me what Slugger's eyes had already conveyed.

The cancer we'd fought successfully for weeks had returned and taken hold. It had already begun spreading rapidly through his body, and now there was little we could do besides try and keep the accompanying pain at bay.

Though the ache in my heart made it hard for me to grasp all the facts, I understood the implications when the doctor said that letting nature take its course would lead to an excruciatingly painful and difficult end to Slugger's life. I knew he deserved better. "Can you keep him comfortable until we can get there?"

"Yeah, Leigh, we'll do that." For a few minutes the two of us cried together. Then Dr. Quatmann sniffed and said, "You're doing what's best for Slugger."

"He gave me his best every day for so many years, how could I not do what's best for him now?" My words came out unclear, broken by emotion, but my resolve was steadfast. Even though it would hurt like hell, I would do right by Slugger. I would call Pranav, and the two of us would return to Roanoke Animal Hospital to say our final goodbyes.

When we reached the hospital, we were ushered

quietly into one of the back exam rooms. The door was ajar and few moments later, I heard a commotion. I peered down the hall. Lo and behold, there was Slugger!

With his IV still attached and hospital staff breaking into a jog to keep up with him, my dying dog was *running* to me. "That run," said Dr. Quatmann as she walked in and wiped the tears from her eyes, "was just like Slugger, all heart."

I wrapped my arms around him then and tried to listen as the doctor gently explained the procedure. She assured me Slugger would feel no pain, he would just drift off to sleep peacefully. But for a while we all sat on the floor and petted him; we talked about what a loving, helpful, wise, absolutely remarkable being he was.

I knew I'd been blessed to share a journey with him. And now I also knew I had to let him go. Tears streamed down my face when I nodded to Dr. Quatmann. I wanted the last voice my beloved dog heard to be my own.

As he fell into his deep and final sleep I whispered the words of the nightly promise I'd shared with him since our very first night together so many years ago: "Rest well, my sweet dog. I love you." Only this time I couldn't add, "I'll see you in the morning." Instead I whispered, "Thank you, dear Slugger, thank you, thank you, thank you, thank you."

Then his heart stopped beating.

Chapter 17

Abiding Memories

I wasn't sure how I'd make it through that first night without Slugger. For weeks I'd stayed up with him, watching him, tending to him, doing whatever I could to help my beloved dog through the long dark hours.

And now, here I was facing another night—but this time, the long dark hours were mine to endure without him. Slugger, I knew, was free of his pain. I was comforted by the realization that he was finally at peace. But that comfort wasn't deep enough for my own pain.

I felt as if the heart within me had shattered when Slugger's stopped, and by morning a single aching question was all that remained in its place. Restless and unsure what to do, I pulled my ragged self out of bed. Kenda trotted into the room to greet me.

She grabbed a shoe in accordance with the game she'd learned from Slugger. Then she put it down and just stood there, looking up at me. Her uncertainty seemed to mirror my own.

Together Kenda and I ventured slowly into the front room. I collapsed onto the couch and instinctively looked over to where Slugger's bed was situated. The site of it there—empty—was more than I could take.

Though I thought my red and swollen eyes couldn't possibly make any more tears than they'd offered over the last twenty-four hours, now I was crying again. Shifting my gaze to the floor, I whispered the question that echoed within me.

"What will I do without you?" I needed to speak that question, to give it voice. I needed to feel as if Slugger, in some way, might hear it.

When I lifted my eyes, I couldn't help wondering if he had. As I turned to look at his bed, I saw a rainbow. It stretched across the brown cushion and toward the living room window as perfectly as if some unseen artist had painted it there.

For a long moment I simply stared. Then the voice of logic in my head said, *This is a figment of your over-stressed brain.* I rubbed my eyes and blinked hard. The rainbow remained.

Perhaps it was merely the product of a beam of sunlight shining coincidentally through the glass panel of the front door. Perhaps it was something more. To me, the colorful arc was beyond beautiful; it soothed the jagged edges of my broken heart like a salve.

I got down on the floor then, next to Slugger's bed. Taking a deep, cleansing breath, I suddenly began to imagine my beloved first dog not as I'd last seen him, but healed, happy.

Kenda came up and sat beside me. "Well, girlie," I whispered, "You reckon our boy's in a place where there are lots of bedside socks to nab? There better be gobs of cheese there, too. And oh yeah, let's not forget the manure piles! How much you want to bet he's already romping in one?" I said, chuckling for the first time in weeks.

Kenda twitched her tail at the sound of my laughter. A moment later she lay down. The pretty little dog's right front paw rested at the edge of Slugger's bed. Now the rainbow fell across that paw, wrapping her yellow fur in a sparkling band of color.

How fitting, I thought. Given the bond that had grown between Kenda and her mentor, I knew that she needed comforting now too. I wrapped my arms around her and held her tight.

Kenda and I shared many such hugs in the weeks and months that followed. Though I was grateful for the caring support of many friends and family members, it was my sensitive girl Lab who helped heal my broken heart most of all. Her sweet ways, dedicated assistance, and funny antics brought me a comfort far deeper than words.

That comfort remains steadfast—even now, five years after Slugger's passing. At the moment Kenda is asleep beneath my desk as I write. She's snoring like a diminutive freight train, and her long, curly whiskers brush lightly against my bare foot, tickling me. The practical, deadline-oriented voice in my mind says, *Wake her, ask her to find another napping spot so that you can work without disruption.*

This time my heart overrules. I love watching my cute little Lab. She's dreaming now. Her right front paw twitches, and a muted bark wells up from her throat. Her tail thwacks repeatedly against the carpet.

I wonder what this good dream is about. Is she running after a well-thrown tennis ball? Dashing to find her favorite stuffed duck? Maybe. But as I gaze down at Kenda, I'd rather believe that her thoughts, like my own, have turned to the Lab we both loved, the one who forever changed my life.

Perhaps in her dream Kenda is racing joyfully across a sunlit meadow. And beside her is a dog named Slugger.

Readers' Guide Discussion Questions

Overall: Would you consider *A Dog Named Slugger* more of a 'dog story' or one of the author's personal growth? In your opinion, did the historical stories, where the author recalled scenes from childhood, add to the story as a whole, or were you more drawn to the immediate relationship between Leigh and Slugger?

1. What new insights did *A Dog Named Slugger* provide about the physical, emotional, and social impact of living with cerebral palsy? What did you learn about service dog partnership that you didn't know before?

2. In the beginning of the book, Leigh visits the doctor for stress fractures in her feet. She writes, "The silver-haired specialist told me not to worry. He said I was so beautiful that I wouldn't have any trouble finding a nice man to take care of me." What does this suggest about the physician's opinion of his patient? What do you think motivated him to see her in this way? In this scene, the author goes on to write, "I bristled. *What does a nice man have to do with the pain in my feet? I thought. And who says I can't take care of myself?*" How do you think the interaction between the patient and physician might have changed if Leigh had voiced her thoughts?

3. When Leigh meets Anne Cooper and her service dog, Caesar, she is able to let go of her usual denial and be

truthful about needing help. How is this positive experience repeated with others as the story unfolds?

4. The author writes, "As a child I'd been taught to keep my CP a secret. I didn't talk about it or even say its name." Compare the lack of physical control experienced by the character with the emotional control she had to exert to accomplish this.

5. How is Sylvia's input regarding Leigh's disability different from the input she receives from those in the medical field? From others in her life? How does this difference influence Leigh's sense of self? How does it influence her relationships with others?

6. The author writes, "Sylvia understood that some gifts must change hands in order to change a life." What does this mean to you? How does the gift of Slugger continue to change Leigh's life and the lives of others?

7. Discuss the rewards and challenges of raising and training a service dog and then letting it go. Is this something you could do? When have you seen the life-changing power of sacrifice in your own life?

8. Leigh says, "For so long, keeping up with others had been my definition of grace." What do you think this means? How does Slugger enable Leigh to eventually re-define grace for herself? What is your own definition of grace? Has this changed in your life? What inspired that change?

9. Slugger's trainer advises Leigh not to expect her new partner to act like a person or a machine since he is neither. What specific dog traits make Leigh's initial training with Slugger especially challenging? Which

canine tendencies make it rewarding?

10. During their first 'lunch date' together, Slugger shows Leigh that the purest devotion can pass from one heart to another without a sound. Discuss the impact that devotion has on Leigh's life and her sense of self. Have you experienced similar devotion in your own life?

11. It took Slugger two years and countless hours of training to become a service dog. What lessons did Leigh have to learn in order to work with him effectively? About the dog? About herself? About working as a team?

12. The author often mentions not being able to control her own body. How does Slugger offer her a sense of control physically, emotionally, socially? How does Leigh's changed perception of her autonomy influence other people's responses to her?

13. How do Leigh's medical experiences as a child create a fear of ridicule that she feels as a young adult? How does her partnership with Slugger enable her to gradually overcome this?

14. The author writes: "As a child, I was never sure of myself; instead I'd been convinced of my own weirdness. I'd been told that because of my disability I had to be not only tough, but also better than other people. This, I'd believed, was my redemption, a chance to make amends for my weirdness. When I was little, I was a dynamo of compensation. I made straight A's. I made jokes. I earned a reputation as one of the best-behaved kids in my school." How does this drive for perfection shape Leigh's training and eventual partnership with Slugger? How does Slugger

gradually change Leigh's belief that she has to be 'better' than others?

15. Leigh recounts a situation at graduate school when she is preparing to go down a set of stairs with Slugger's assistance. "My dog looked up at me. His brown eyes sparkled with a sure and simple message, "Take hold." How does the Labrador inspire his partner to learn to 'take hold' of other aspects of her life?

16. What message is Leigh given about her sexuality as she grows up? Do you think this reflects a societal attitude about disability and sexuality? How is this attitude evident in the author's college experience with another disabled student, Joe? Do you think a similar attitude exists in society today?

17. *A Dog Named Slugger* highlights many instances where the author faces biased attitudes regarding her physical disability. How are these instances similar to the cultural bias she discovers in forming a relationship with Pranav, a man from India? How are they different?

18. Slugger enables personal growth for Leigh by encouraging her independence, assertiveness, and sense of control. What benefits does the dog eventually bring to Pranav, and to the relationship that develops between him and the author? Do you consider a pet part of your own family? What rewards and difficulties does this bring to your life?

19. Which of Slugger's attributes makes it possible for him to positively influence the clients with mental disabilities with whom Leigh works? Have you ever experienced a unique bond or sense of healing from

an animal unlike what you experience with other people?

20. When working at Ronald McDonald House, the author writes that Slugger's message to cancer patients is: "You are more than pain, more than worry, more than cancer. You are you. And you are good." How does he share this same message with Leigh? Compare this message with those Leigh encountered growing up.

21. Do you believe Leigh's experience of employment discrimination is rare, or do individuals with disabilities continue to face barriers to employment today?

22. Near the end of the legal battle over Leigh's right to be accompanied by Slugger in the workplace, she wonders if it has all been worth it. What do you think? What choice would you make if you found yourself in that situation?

23. Leigh says her friend Carol has Milkbones in her lemonade because she's made something positive out of her struggle and gone on to help others with disabilities get service dogs. How does Leigh learn to do this in her own life? Have you faced challenges and responded to them in ways that were positive for you and/or for other people?

24. How might Leigh's decision not to ask Slugger to work while in pain have been influenced by her early experiences denying and ignoring her own physical pain? Can you identify with the inclination to give loved ones a level of care we may deny ourselves?

25. How does the decision to bring a second service dog, Kenda, into their lives effect Leigh, Slugger, and Pranav? Can you relate to the joys and challenges of this decision?

26. How does Leigh's final goodbye to Slugger in the veterinarian's office demonstrate the strength of their bond? How is Slugger's strength evident? What strength does Leigh show? Have you ever had to decide if or when to put a beloved pet to sleep? What factors guided your decision?

28. Leigh's final words to Slugger are, "Thank you, dear Slugger, thank you, thank you, thank you, thank you." What do you think she is thanking him for?

29. On the morning after Slugger's death, Leigh sees a rainbow across his empty bed. She writes, "Perhaps it was merely the product of a beam of sunlight shining coincidentally through the glass panel of the front door. Perhaps it was something more." What do you think?

About the Author

Image by L. Jeffery

Leigh Brill is a writer, speaker, and advocate for people with disabilities. She published her first story at the age of fifteen; since then her writing has reached national and international audiences through publications including *Chicken Soup to Inspire the Body & Soul*, the Guideposts book *Soul Menders*, and the magazines *Just Labs: A Celebration of the Labrador Retriever* and *Pets: Part of the Family*. Leigh has shared more than a decade of her life in the company of service dogs and continues to do so. She lives with her family in rural Virginia.

Visit her at www.leighbrill.com.

Photo Gallery
Leigh, Slugger and Kenda

For years I struggled with physical, emotional, and social challenges. I couldn't find a single good thing about having to live with cerebral palsy . . . until I met Slugger.

**An early practice session with me,
Slugger, and trainer Vickie Polk.**

Courtesy *The Daily News-Record,* photo by Allen Litten.

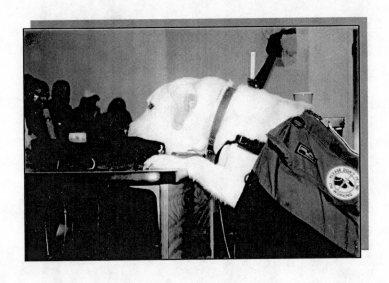

Slugger loved retrieving my nylon pack; he was a true service dog, who enjoyed his job.

Laundry was one of Slugger's favorite household chores.

My constant companion was vigilant even during car trips.

Slugger
adored
his Pooh
bear toy!

Slugger's
working pack
was a
testament to
his training.
The sparkle
in his eye was
a testament to
his spirit.

Life wasn't all about work for Slugger. A good ball and some open space was all it took to bring out his playful side.

How we loved our quiet times together in the sun!

Slugger and I found moments for affection even in the midst of our busiest days.

Kenda, the little 'Audrey Hepburn dog', charmed me from the day we met!

Image by M. Tinaglia

Service dogs are more than working partners. As Kenda's bond with Pranav proves, they are a vital part of our family.

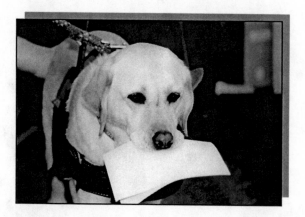

As Slugger transitioned into retirement, Kenda proved herself worthy of his legacy. Mail call! Kenda is happy to carry anything, even fragile envelopes, when asked. *Image by S. DeBruycker*

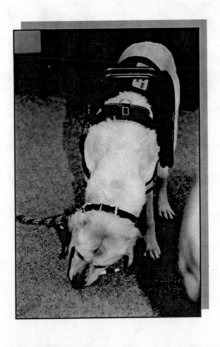

Dressed in her working packs and harness, Kenda is a writer's best friend, eager to retrieve my pen whenever I drop it.

Image by S. DeBruycker

Kenda quickly picked up Slugger's talent for impressing school kids when we demonstrate our teamwork. Like Slugger before her, Kenda often joins me to encourage awareness and appreciation of service dog teams.

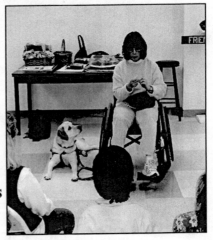

Here I am with Kenda and Slugger, my double blessings. Kenda became his helpmate just as he'd become mine.

Kenda and I shared hugs and healing after Slugger's death.

Image by N. Patriarco

Shortly after we said goodbye to Slugger, my husband captured this image of Kenda. Like the rainbow that appeared the morning after my first canine partner died, this beautiful picture reminds me that the goodness Slugger shared remains with us always.

It would be nearly impossible for me to list every service dog training organization and disability-related resource in existence today. The brief list provided here is intended as a starting point to encourage further understanding and appreciation of service dogs and the people whose lives they touch.

❖ A portion of the proceeds from sales of A Dog Named Slugger will go to support the life-changing work of **Saint Francis Service Dogs**. To learn more about the foundation, contact:

Saint Francis Service Dogs
PO Box 19538
Roanoke VA 24019
Email: info@saintfrancisdogs.org
Or visit: http://www.saintfrancisdogs.org

❖ If you'd like more information about service dogs, including a list of organizations that place them across the United States and internationally, contact **Assistance Dogs International, Inc.** ADI is a coalition of not-for-profit organizations that train and place assistance dogs. The purpose of ADI is to improve the areas of training, placement, and utilization of assistance dogs as well as staff and volunteer education. To reach ADI, contact:

Assistance Dogs International
P.O. Box 5174
Santa Rosa, California 95402
www.assistancedogsinternational.org

❖ To explore online resources, articles, and a helpful list of web links related to working dogs, visit: **www.workingdogs.com,** the international magazine for and about working and sporting dogs— and the people who love them.

❖ For information and technical assistance on the **Americans with Disabilities Act** (including information about legal aspects of assistance animal partnership), visit the ADA home page on the web at: www.ADA.gov

❖ **United Cerebral Palsy (UCP)'s** mission is to advance the independence, productivity and full citizenship of people with disabilities through an affiliate network. Learn more at: www.ucp.org.

❖ **DailyStrength** offers free and anonymous online support group communities where hundreds of thousands of members share advice and encouragement. For more information, go to: www.dailystrength.org.

LaVergne, TN USA
07 July 2010
188610LV00002B/1/P